‑ ‑ ⁓UE

James McGill is well known as the founder of McGill University, but the rest of his accomplishments remain little known. This new biography reveals the fascinating life story of a man who, as fur trader, merchant, public servant, and colonel of the militia, played a significant role in Canada's development.

McGill came to Canada from Scotland in 1766 at the age of twenty-two. After the years as a fur trader, he moved to Montreal and co-founded Todd, McGill and Co. He continued in the fur trade but also encouraged general trade and in later years pioneered the export of goods to Britain. Active in politics, McGill was a magistrate of Montreal and a member of the first parliament of Lower Canada. He also served for many years as a member of the Governor's Executive Council. During the War of 1812 he commanded the militia that defended Montreal, helping to foil the United States' attempts to annex Canada.

Educated at Glasgow University, McGill never lost his love of learning, and his bequest of land and an endowment to found a college bearing his name was a gesture fully consistent with his generous character and strong commitment to the city he had made his own.

STANLEY BRICE FROST is director of the History of McGill Project, McGill University.

James McGill of Montreal

STANLEY BRICE FROST

McGill-Queen's University Press
Montreal & Kingston • London • Buffalo

© McGill-Queen's University Press 1995
ISBN 0-7735-1296-9 (cloth)
ISBN 0-7735-1297-7 (paper)

Legal deposit third quarter 1995
Bibliothèque nationale du Québec

Printed in Canada on acid-free paper

McGill-Queen's University Press is grateful to the Canada Council for
support of its publishing program.

Publication of this book has been made possible by grants from the
F. Cyril James Fund, the James McGill Society, and a matching donation
from Gordon J. Wasserman, BA, 1959, generosities that are recorded
with gratitude and appreciation.

Canadian cataloguing in publication data

Frost, Stanley Brice
  James McGill of Montreal
  ISBN 0-7735-1296-9 (bound) –
  ISBN 0-7735-1297-7 (pbk.)
  1. McGill, James, 1744–1813. 2. McGill University – Biography.
  3. Montréal (Quebec) – Biography.   4. Quebec (Province) –
  Biography.   5. Quebec (Province) – Politics and government –
  1791–1841.   I. Title.
  FC2947.26.M34F76 1995 378.714'28   F1054.5.M853F76   1995

This book was typeset by Typo Litho Composition Inc.
in 10.5/13 Palatino.

This book is dedicated with respect and affection to
Miss Maysie Steele MacSporran, BA, 1927, MA, 1930
Honorary life member, James McGill Society, 1993
and first biographer of James McGill

Contents

Illustrations and Maps

Preface

In 1870, a little more than fifty years after McGill's death, Principal William Dawson, in a lecture entitled "James McGill and the Origin of His University," could give only the bare outline of McGill's life and two small contributions of aged persons who could recall details they had heard about McGill in their youth – that he enjoyed singing voyageur songs and liked to read books. Fifty years later again, celebrating the university's charter centenary with a history, Dean Cyrus Macmillan had to write: "Only meagre facts about the life of James McGill are available, and documentary evidence bearing on his career is scanty."

In the late nineteen-twenties, however, matters took a turn for the better. Judge E. Fabre Surveyer published in the Montreal newspaper *La Presse* a series of biographical sketches of members of Lower Canada's first Legislative Assembly, including one of James McGill. This he expanded in English into a paper read to the Canadian Historical Society and published in the *McGill News* in 1929. It was not so much a biographical sketch as a listing of items gleaned from various legal archives, but added materially to the volume of known McGill facts. Another immense treasure trove opened up that same year when Milton M. Quaife began publishing the John Askin papers, which included much correspondence between Askin and McGill, and also with the Todd, McGill Company.

Gradually, then, more pieces of the mosaic were emerging from the past, but the only person to attempt to put them together into a biographical whole was Miss Maysie MacSporran. She did this in 1928–30, when not all the newest fragments were available to her, but there were enough to delineate the first coherent portrait of a remarkable personality, a man of great interest in his own right, quite apart from his benefaction for a college. For her excellent presentation she was awarded the master of arts degree by McGill University, and sixty years later she still deserves recognition as the pioneer. This book could not be dedicated to any other.

Milton Quaife's contribution to McGill studies was further enriched with the publication of a second volume of Askin correspondence in 1934. In the 1930s, the antiquarian W.D. Lighthall found in an old desk three little almanac volumes for the years 1801, 1802, and 1812, containing brief weather and garden jottings by James McGill and, by great good fortune, diary-style notes of events at two notable moments in his later years. Lighthall also bought from a farmer a fascinating volume, the financial daybook of the James and Andrew McGill Company for the years 1798 to 1800, with financial summaries of later years. But Lighthall also told the melancholy tale of "old Mdme Desrivières in her dotage" burning "most of the [McGill] books and papers in the yard of the manor house" in the Eastern Townships, sometime in the late 1890s.

Since 1940 more information has come to light from a McGill family history researched and written in Scotland, and from archives and libraries that surrendered items, sometimes small in themselves but significant for the emerging portrait. Our own university library acquired a number of business letters relating to land in the Eastern Townships as well as McGill's cashbook for the years 1809–15. Much general information has emerged from the growing interest in eighteenth-century commerce generally. However, since Miss MacSporran's thesis was never published, James McGill has remained unknown to the general public, forgotten except in name, obscured by the university of which he was *fons et origo*.

The present book is an attempt to use all the information now available – by no means all presented here, but represented by necessary selection – to offer the portrait of a man who emerges as courageous, hard working, shrewd, warmly benevolent in personal relationships, strongly endowed with gifts of leadership, and public spirited to a truly remarkable degree. He was also sensitive to and sympathetic with French Canadien aspirations. Montreal and the province of Quebec owe much to one who enriched, administered, and defended his city and served his country well in critical years.

I have large debts to acknowledge, first, of course, to Miss Mac-Sporran and then to Milton Quaife and W.D. Lighthall, and to the great historians of Canada and the fur trade on whose works I have depended, always with respect and gratitude. Particular recognition must be given to Professor John Cooper for his informative article on James McGill in the *Dictionary of Canadian Biography*. I have to thank as always those two great research services, the staffs of the McLennan Library Reference Department and of the McGill University Archives. Their patience is as inexhaustible as their resources. I thank Professors John Brierley of the Faculty of Law, Margaret Gillett of the Faculty of Education, Carman Miller of the History Department, and Peter McNally of the School of Library and Information Studies for their very helpful comments on drafts of the manuscript.

I am indebted to David Widgington of the Department of Geography at Concordia University for producing the historical maps of Quebec boundaries, and particularly to artist Jane Kingsland of the McGill Archives for drawing McGill's Beaver Club medal and redrawing Lieutenant Buckland's canoe sketch. I also thank Pauline Lahache for her kind permission to use the map of Lac St Louis. The drawing by James Duncan was provided by the McGill Archives. All other illustrations have been generously supplied by the Lawrence M. Lande Foundation for Historical Canadian Research of the McLennan Library of McGill University. I acknowledge with gratitude the interest of Dr Lande and the invaluable help of the Lande Librarian, Mrs Nellie Reis. Mrs Véronique Schami and Mrs Kathryn Hubbard have been more than generous with their time and talents in the production of the manuscript; I thank them sincerely.

Something more than formal thanks, however sincere, must be expressed to Principal David Johnston. From the beginning he has encouraged me in this task, read drafts of the manuscript as he went to and fro in the earth (one came back to me from Alexandria, Egypt, liberally supplied with meticulous notes), and has regularly enquired as to its progress. Writing a book is necessarily a lonely task; I trust David knows how much his support has meant to me.

Stanley Brice Frost
April, 1995

James McGill of Montreal

1 The Young Adventurer, 1744–66

The little knot of men busy on the wooden landing stage at Lachine, ten miles up river from Montréal, were readily recognizable
by their broad, woven belts, the colourful ceintures fléchées, as
Canadiens of Nouvelle France. Behind these workers lay the long,
sturdy log hut where Indian goods for the fur trade had been
stored. They had been brought overland from the warehouses of
the city since this was still the only way around the turbulent Lachine Rapids. Now the men were bringing out the goods, divided
into packs weighing some ninety pounds apiece, and stowing
them carefully in the half a dozen great forty-foot canoes lined up
beside the wharf or waiting their turn down river close to the
bank.

The sun shone warmly this early May morning in the year 1766.
Some of the crew members were already taking off their deerskin
jackets and folding them down where they would provide welcome knee padding once the paddling began. One of them, as
sturdily built as his fellows but some two or three inches taller and
with a fairer, more northern colouring, was preparing the place assigned to him amidships in the leading canoe, where the brigade
captain could keep a wary eye upon him. He spoke little to his
companions and seemed to have no well wishers in the group of
wives, bonnes amies, and friends who had come this far to see the
voyageurs depart and to wish them Godspeed on their perilous
journey. The fact was, the young man had not yet learned enough

of the local language to converse easily – it sounded quite unlike the French he remembered from his school days – and his only acquaintance in Montréal was the fellow Scot who had hired him as his factor in this enterprise and given him his last instructions and advice back in the city. The raw hand knew his future companions would all be watching closely to see how this foreigner, a newcomer to the complex and dangerous business of fur trading, was going to make out. No doubt he was anxiously asking himself the same question, but if so, he did not let it show in his face. He laid his musket down beside him in the bottom of the canoe, touched the knife and hatchet at his belt to assure himself they were in place, settled into position, and waited for the bowman to take his place and give the command *En avant*. If he recalled at that moment that the woodsman's knife was universally termed a scalping knife, he did not let the implications deter him.

He was not such a greenhorn as some of his companions might have thought. He had spent five or six years knocking about in the Carolinas before coming north to try his luck in the Canadian fur trade. To get to Montréal, he had taken ship from Charleston to New York, an easy voyage, but had then joined a party journeying four hundred miles, first up the Hudson River to the falls, portaging overland to Lake George, and then following the great lake and river system through Lac Champlain and the Richelieu until he reached St Jean. There he finally debarked for the twenty-mile hike to the St Lawrence and the Indian ferry to Montréal. Anyone who had accomplished that journey could reckon himself a pretty experienced woods and canoe man – but that, his new companions assured him in their thick patois, was nothing to what faced him now: an adventure of six or seven weeks of continual paddling, first up the Ottawa, then across country by creeks and lakes and trails to Lake Nipissing, then again across country to Lake Huron, along the shores of Georgian Bay, league after league of paddling, sometimes through calm but often rough water, and so finally to Michilimackinac, the meeting place of Lakes Huron, Michigan, and Superior and the great assembly point for Indians and fur traders alike. All this to penetrate deep into the western wilderness, five hundred miles as the crow flies but more than double that distance by canoe. The travellers would be isolated from even the rudiments of civilization by an ever-increasing expanse of forest and water, with no possible assistance in time of

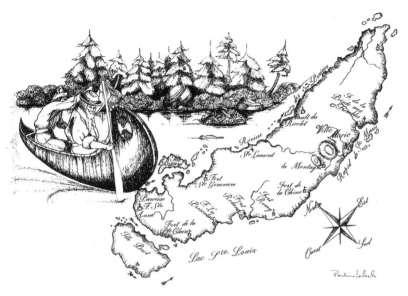

Detail from Bellin's map of Lake St Louis, 1744. Artist Pauline Lahache.

trouble except that of your comrades. Nor could there be any turning back. Once you took your place in one of those great trading canoes you were committed for at least four months, the duration of the journey out and back, and if you were foolhardy enough to attempt to winter in the wilderness, as this young man had contracted to do, it would be a year or more before you saw again the frontier settlement of Montréal. It was an adventure to make even the stoutest heart recoil, but the young man had thought the matter through and had made his decision. He was not going to turn back now. With his face set, he grasped his paddle and took position. As the voyageurs pushed off from the dock and dipped their paddles for the the first leg of their journey up Lac St Louis, they broke into a Canadien boatsong, and a Scottish voice, melodious and deep, joined in, often muffing the words but getting the note and the stroke right. The young man was twenty-two years old and his name was James McGill.

James McGill was born in Glasgow, Scotland, on 6 October 1744, into a household of modest but respectable resources. The family was one of a number in the city bearing that name, and the progenitors of the clan, according to the family historian, John

Michael McGill,[1] had been prominent in Galloway, an area to the southwest of Glasgow, since the twelfth century. But the immediate forebears of James McGill are thought to have removed to Glasgow some time in the seventeenth century and to have become established townsfolk; certainly, the men of the family were known as respected tradesmen and burghers at least two generations before our James McGill appeared on the scene.

His grandfather was the first James McGill in his line of whom there is documentary evidence. This James I is on record as having married Janet, daughter of James Craig, hammerman, on 7 June 1716, and as having been admitted as a member of the Guild of Hammermen and burghers of the city on 11 September following. There is evidence to suggest that he was apprenticed to James Craig, and if so, he married his master's daughter just prior to gaining full qualification in his craft. The couple's first child, a boy, was also named James; he was born on 7 April 1717, and twenty-four years later he too was admitted to the Guild of Hammermen and acknowledged as a burgher of Glasgow. James McGill II was, in one regard at least, a little more circumspect than his father, for in 1742 he married Margaret Gibson a few months after his completion of indenture rather than before it. His first child was a daughter, Janet, but his second child was a boy, christened James like his father and grandfather, and it was this James McGill who would later become founder of the university bearing his name.[2] Thus, his father, grandfather, and maternal great-grandfather were all named James, all practised the same craft, and were all members of the Guild of Hammermen.

This craft association, the Incorporated Guild of Hammermen, gives a glimpse into the everyday life of eighteenth-century Glasgow. The city still regulated its commerce and industry by the medieval system of incorporated guilds, and only members in good standing of the appropriate guild were permitted to ply their trade or craft within the city limits.[3] Membership of a guild also conferred burgher status and thus carried obligations of proper conduct not only in the practice of the craft but also in such matters as conforming to the magistrates' ordinances, assisting the forces of law and order in time of riot, helping in fire fighting, and sharing in the defence of the city should it be attacked. James McGill, it should be noted, grew up familiar with the idea that citizenship conferred both privileges and responsibilities.

THE McGILL FAMILY TREE

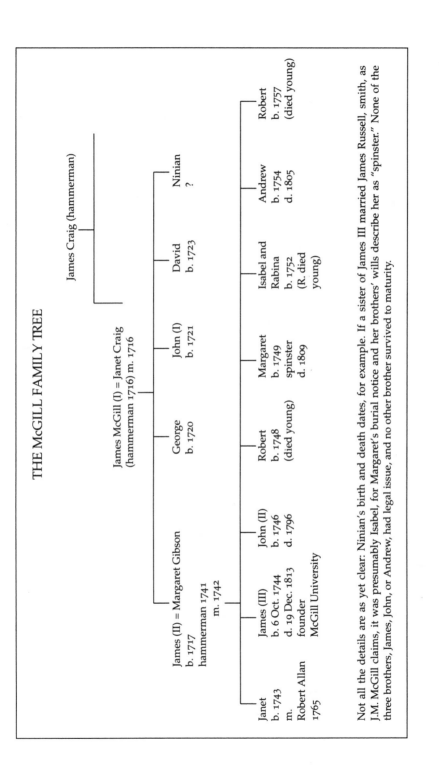

James Craig (hammerman)

James McGill (I) = Janet Craig
(hammerman 1716) m. 1716

George
b. 1720

John (I)
b. 1721

David
b. 1723

Ninian
?

James (II) = Margaret Gibson
b. 1717
hammerman 1741
m. 1742

Janet
b. 1743
m.
Robert Allan
1765

James (III)
b. 6 Oct. 1744
d. 19 Dec. 1813
founder
McGill University

John (II)
b. 1746
d. 1796

Robert
b. 1748
(died young)

Margaret
b. 1749
spinster
d. 1809

Isabel and
Rabina
b. 1752
(R. died
young)

Andrew
b. 1754
d. 1805

Robert
b. 1757
(died young)

Not all the details are as yet clear: Ninian's birth and death dates, for example. If a sister of James III married James Russell, smith, as J.M. McGill claims, it was presumably Isabel, for Margaret's burial notice and her brothers' wills describe her as "spinster." None of the three brothers, James, John, or Andrew, had legal issue, and no other brother survived to maturity.

The members of the Guild of Hammermen were in fact iron-smiths, practitioners of a craft and trade that encompassed far more than the activities of blacksmiths today. Iron and early forms of steel, produced in small one- or two-men smithies, were extensively used in buildings, in decorative displays, and for a host of utility articles from fencing and gates to weapons, pots and pans, brooches, and pins. The farrier's business was only a small part, if any, of the hammerman's activities, and James McGill II is mentioned at least twice in city records as having carried out "iron-work" on municipal property. He was evidently a man of some energy and initiative, for in 1755 he was elected deacon of the guild and served for two years.[4] Six years earlier he had begun to acquire property in Stockwell Street, and in the early 1760s he acquired more land and erected "tenements," as they were called, or apartment buildings, in one of which he and his family lived while renting out the rest. In the later years of the decade he acquired still more property and was in possession of buildings on both sides of Stockwell Street.

James II was twenty-seven years old when his son, James III, was born and as the boy grew up, the prosperity of the father increased, to the point where young James was sent to Glasgow Grammar School, the precursor of the present Glasgow High School. The hours of study were very long, commencing at 5 A.M. most of the year and at 7 A.M. in winter, and lasting until about five or six in the evening, with two intervals for meals. Punishments were severe and the cane very much in evidence. Most schools had a large boulder or block of stone near the door, which was called the "cooling stane," and after the boys were caned they sat on this stone, the coldness of which was supposed to counteract the pain of the punishment. "Truly," John McGill commented, "the children's lot in the seventeenth and eighteenth century was far from being a happy one."[5] James had probably little reason to recall his schooldays with nostalgia.

In the grammar school, the boy studied just what the name implies – grammar, Latin grammar. He needed that to enter the university, but what else he was taught in school – a little arithmetic, possibly some simple geometry – we do not know. It is doubtful whether he received, either at school or in the university, any formal instruction in the use of the English language. In the eighteenth century, education at the University of Glasgow was oriented (as everywhere else in Europe at that time) wholly to the classical inheritance, that is, Latin and Greek literature, including mathematics, logic, and Aristotelian natural philosophy. McGill's curriculum would also have included some divinity and probably, as an optional subject, some French, especially if he already had it in mind to seek a commercial career. His education was certainly not intended to be a preparation for "the real world," but it did mightily exercise his brain, discipline his thinking, and teach him to express himself. In later life he proved himself able to write clear, forceful prose, setting out in good order his argument on matters of considerable complexity. Moreover, his education gave him not only a sense of history, which is the hallmark of an educated person, but also in his later career the franchise of the world of officialdom and the ruling classes: he could recognize both a classical allusion and the style of imperial governments and their consuls in the provinces.

On the practical side, his education equipped him with the ability to master merchant-style accounting and current financial methods, the niceties of legal commitments and the practices of the courts of law. He also had the ability and the interest to read and appreciate some of the important books of his day and to improve his French to the point where he became comfortably bilingual. His education evidently meant much to him personally, for he became an early and persistent advocate of the provision of English schooling in his adopted country. That he left the university without graduating conformed to the general practice of the day. He probably reached the stage where to go further would indicate an intention to enter one of the "learned professions," that is, law, medicine, schoolmastering, or the Church. Such a life was not for James McGill. He preferred something more vigorous, more venturesome, more exciting. He was to find it in full measure.

In the matriculation album of the University, James III was described as "Jacobus McGill, filius natu maximus Jacobi mercatoris Glasguensis," that is as the son of a "merchant" rather than "hammerman," signalling that with increased prosperity his father was rising socially, a fact confirmed by his sending both James and his younger brother Andrew, not into the family craft, but to college. It also suggests a motivation for James's own commercial aspirations. John, the intervening brother, may not have done so well as his siblings at the grammar-school stage, for he did not matriculate into the university, but he too received enough education to be able to operate modestly in later years as a merchant in Canada. It is noteworthy that none of James II's sons followed him into the craft of hammermen. However, the family may not have wholly lost touch with the smithy, for one of James III's sisters is said to have married "James Russel, smith," in 1772. But the male younger generation, James, John, and Andrew, were all ready to say farewell to their father's and grandfathers' way of life and launch out into the world in search of better and more rewarding living. In this, not only by right of primogeniture but also by force of character, James III was the leader, as he was to be in all the brothers' affairs.

James came to maturity at a time of exciting new possibilities. The Americas on the far side of the Atlantic had been the land of opportunity for young Europeans for two hundred and fifty years, but Spain, Portugal, and France had at first enjoyed a rich monopoly. Then in the early seventeenth century England established its own North American colonies, and these had flourished for a century and a half. Scotland was slower off the mark. Attempts had been made as early as 1621 to found Nova Scotia in the Acadian peninsula but the venture was so poorly supported that in 1632 the area was traded back to France.[6] Led by William Patterson, Scots in the late seventeenth century attempted to set up their own trading colony on the Isthmus of Darien, but the scheme foundered disastrously owing to the climate, disease, and Spanish hostility. Merchants had invested heavily in this venture and it was said that half the wealth of Scotland was wiped out by its failure. At that point, the English government proposed the parliamentary union of the two kingdoms, England and Scotland; they had shared the same sovereign for a century, ever since the accession of James VI of Scotland as James I of England. Part of the proposal – the only attractive part as many Scots saw it – was that England would buy up the stock of the failed Darien Company and open its colonies in North America to Scots as freely as to her own nationals. From 1707, the date of the Act of Union, Glasgow, the main Scottish gateway to the West, began quickly to grow and prosper.[7] Scottish merchants turned their attention to the business of growing and marketing tobacco, and rich "tobacco lords," as they came to be known, became a familiar and influential element in Glaswegian society. Young men in mid-eighteenth-century Scotland, rebelling against the lack of opportunities at home, now had a rich and promising field of adventure beckoning them to cross the Atlantic and make their fortunes.

At what age James McGill made the decision to sail we do not know, since no detailed immigration records for the period 1740–73 are extant. There is a tradition, for which so far no supporting evidence has been found, that James was accompanied from the beginning by his brother John (who was only two years his junior) and that they made their way first to the flourishing tobacco-growing colonies of the Carolinas, which sounds a sensible, indeed obvious, thing to do. If James left the university at age sixteen there are six or so years to be accounted for before he first arrived in Montréal, and the likeliest scenario is that some of those years were indeed spent in the southern English colonies. But McGill clearly did not find there the opportunity he was seeking: possibly the climate was too hot and humid for a northern-bred lad, and possibly also the English social climate was also not congenial to one whose pronounced Scottish accent was as undiluted as his Scottish character and outlook. The "bon ton" society of the Carolinas prided itself on its English fashions and social distinctions, as John Wesley had discovered to his dismay in Savannah some thirty years earlier. Nor were McGill's compatriots, the Glaswegian tobacco lords and their representatives, overwelcoming to one of their own manifesting an ambition to become a competitor. Without capital behind him to get started, a young man like James McGill could expect the Carolinas to offer only labouring work or at best a lowly clerking position, and he had not come so far from home to be content with such meagre pickings. He quietly accumulated some earnings, but he also looked around for something more promising and exciting. He heard that it was waiting for him in the wilderness that stretched apparently limitlessly west of the frontier town of Montréal in Nouvelle France, up in a northern and as yet (to the British) hardly explored country called Canada.

There the situation was very different from that of the Carolinas. New France had only recently become British territory as the result of military victories in 1759, a turning point in the long struggle between England and France. The Treaty of Paris in 1763 confirmed that all of North America (apart from the fishing islands of St Pierre and Miquelon) from the Carolinas to Newfoundland was now part of Britain's colonial empire. James knew that the major trade of Canada had been in furs, exported from New France through Montréal and Québec to Paris and the markets of Europe. It had been successfully organized by setting up a working partnership of French capitalists, Canadien merchants in Québec City and Montréal, the "coureurs de bois,"[8] and the aboriginal inhabitants, the so-called Indians. But now the talk in the Carolinas was that the British success had deprived the Canadien merchants of their French sources of capital and "Indian goods," which included everything from beads and scalping knives to kettles and guns, and that English but especially Scottish and Irish venturers were stepping in to supply the need. Here was the new opportunity for which James McGill had been looking. A lively, hardy young fellow prepared to risk life and limb in the wilderness could team up with Canadiens who had long since learned the woodscraft, the social patterns, the needs of the Indians, in many cases even their languages, and in time he could himself learn these pathways to wealth. Also, in Montréal he could learn how to arrange matters with the governing English bureaucracy, how to seek out financial backing in Quebec and London, and how to share in opening up new markets in Britain and on the continent of Europe for the abundance of furs the Indians could supply. This kind of business arrangement was one of the things with which he had become familiar during his stay in the Carolinas: capital and manufactured goods flowing out from Britain, raw materials and produce flowing back from the colonies. In Canada the task was to restore the fur trade of the the St Lawrence and the Great Lakes to its former prosperity by providing it with a new network of commercial relationships, British instead of French. James McGill set off from Charleston carrying his small amount of accumulated capital in his money belt, eager to join in the new adventure.

Of course, James, though early off the mark, was not the first to respond to these opportunities. The fact that English colonies were relatively well established and prosperous attracted most British immigration into the Thirteen Colonies; when adventure beckoned in those latitudes it was rather to the west, towards the Ohio. To immigrants from the southern British Isles, the North with its harsh winters was less inviting. But the Scots, and to a lesser degree the Irish, were not so easily deterred, and the Grants, the McGillivrays, the Frobishers, the McTavishes, the Alexander Henrys, the Isaac Todds, and their like had swarmed into Canada, some even before the 1763 treaty decision.

But hard on their heels came James McGill, certainly alone. His brother John did not figure in the Canadian story until later, and then it was as an independent trader. Andrew, the third brother, came two or more years later still and he too set up as an independent trader, though in later years he did become a business partner of James. But it was James who blazed the trail. He was not only courageous and venturesome but was prepared to learn the fur trade the hard way. He is well documented as having passed through Montreal (as the British pronounced the name) in 1766 on his way to Michilimackinac. He is described at that time as a "factor" for a fellow Scot, William Grant,[9] but by agreement with his employer, he laid out his own small fortune in Indian goods and did some small first trading on his own account. He travelled on to Green Bay in what is now Wisconsin on the shore of Lake Michigan, and spent the winter there. To pass a winter in the wilderness and survive to tell the tale was reckoned the supreme test of the fur trader. When he returned to Montreal in the late summer of 1767, James McGill had laid a firm foundation for his subsequent career.

He was described by those who knew him in those days as a tall, strong fellow with a sonorous voice,[10] perhaps two inches short of six feet (average heights in the eighteenth century were less than those of today), somewhat squarely and solidly built, and he tended, we are told, "to corpulence in his later years," a not unusual fate at a time when overeating and overdrinking were much in fashion – though there is no suggestion from his contemporaries that McGill overindulged more than was common. His face according to his portraits was broad and round, with high, arching eyebrows, a rather low forehead, partly, of course, obscured in formal dress by his bob-wig, a nose perhaps a little too large for the face, and a good square chin. It is the face of a practical, shrewd man, a doer as well as a thinker, a man of action, but of actions based on well-principled if rather inflexible opinions. His eyes are those of one who looks on his world with no fear or anxiety, but nonetheless with care and watchfulness. Now that he had come to maturity, James McGill had learned to be a self-assured, self-reliant person.

2 The Fur Trader, 1766–75

The trade into which James McGill was entering so boldly in 1766 had already accumulated a long and varied history, but had suffered a setback in Europe in the earlier part of the sixteenth century largely because overtrapping had depleted available supplies. But when the exploration of North America opened up new sources of fur-bearing animals and particularly of beaver, the fur trade was reinvigorated. The colonization of the more northerly parts of North America was strongly encouraged by the profits gained from the fur trade by both French and, to a more limited extent, English settlers. At the same time the decline of the Mongol nomadic powers allowed Russian explorers to open up the fur-producing lands of Siberia and eventually Alaska. With this increase in supply, the fur trade of Europe revived, furs came into fashion again, and profits grew rapidly. New markets were found in the Middle East and as far away as India and China. The seventeenth and eighteenth centuries were good times for the industry; the English Company of Adventurers Trading into Hudson's Bay was established in 1670 specifically to take advantage of the new opportunities, and the prosperity of the fur trade was still running strongly when in 1766 James McGill took a lowly part in its far-flung activities.

Although fashions and circumstance in Europe dictated the long-term economic fortunes of the fur trade, its pace and its seasons in North America were regulated by the habits of the animals indigenous to the continent's huge forested areas. These constituted the untamed, sparsely inhabited wilderness, as the European colonists termed it. Once the white man began to immigrate in ever increasing numbers, its primitive isolation would be gone forever – within McGill's lifetime areas as far as the Great Lakes were being settled and increasingly exploited. But when he first arrived the wilderness was indeed still the forest primeval, in all its awesome majesty. It was a land of huge distances, immense hardships, and of unforgiving perils, a habitat where only the woodswise and the intrepid could survive. For ten years James McGill learned the ways of the forest and its waters, the habits of its wildlife, the social patterns of its natives, and the patois of the voyageurs.

What lured men into this tapestry of forests and rivers and lakes was the beaver. Other fur-bearing animals such as the marten, the fox, and even the bear were desirable, but the beaver was the staple of the trade.[1] When fully grown this animal weighs up to sixty pounds, and its meat, while rather greasy, was a very acceptable supplement to cornmeal for Indian and fur trader alike. Its fur varies from summer, when it is least valuable, to winter, when it grows more abundantly and is at its best. So winter hunting and trapping were essential, and this set the pattern of the fur trader's activities. Unfortunately, the beaver is a sedentary animal little given to overland migration and so in any area it is easily hunted and soon wiped out.

The European newcomers contributed materially to the massacre of the beaver:

Formerly, the Beavers were very numerous, the many Lakes and Rivers gave them ample space, and the poor Indian had then only a pointed stick shaped and hardened by fire, a stone Hatchet, Spear and Arrowheads of the same; thus armed he was weak against the sagacious Beaver who on the banks of a Lake made itself a house of a foot thick or more; composed of earth and small flat stones, crossed and bound together with pieces of wood; upon which no impression could be made but by fire. But when the Arrival of the White People had changed all their weapons from stone to iron and steel and added the fatal Gun, every animal fell before the Indian … the Beaver became a desirable animal for food and clothing, and the fur itself a valuable article of trade; and as the Beaver is a stationary animal, it could be attacked at any convenient time in all seasons, and thus their numbers became reduced.[2]

Consequently, the hunting grounds for the St Lawrence trade, which in the sixteenth and seventeenth centuries had centred around the Saguenay River, moved steadily westward as traders sought fresh and abundant supplies: in James McGill's early days the centre was in the Great Lakes area but it had moved before his career ended to the far northwest in the foothills of the Rockies. This meant ever lengthening journeys by canoe and portage to reach the hunting grounds and then of course equally long journeys to bring the pelts back to Montreal for shipment to London.

Each ten- to twelve-hour day of those journeys brought its own unremitting demands, including long stretches of paddling, a drudgery rivalled only by the toil of galley slaves. There were also constant irritants from mosquitoes and flies, danger from wild animals, attacks by hostile natives, or life-threatening accidents. Most days there would be portages, when the canoes must be unpacked, transported overland, often through difficult terrain, and refloated when the next creek or lake was reached. The portages also required that the ninety-pound packs of cargo had to be humped two at a time over those same trails, and all the other gear had to be carried as well, so often two or three trips had to be made over distances that could lengthen into miles. Nor were all stretches of water placid streams. Sometimes there would be dangerous rapids or sharp waterfalls to be negotiated. All this had to be accomplished for six or seven weeks on a meagre daily allowance of one quart of cornmeal flavoured with two ounces of hog fat. The fur trader may have found his motivation in the hope of large profits, but for the ordinary voyageur his modest wage could hardly have been the driving force. He found his strength in the freedom of the woods, the challenge to his pride, and the sense of brotherhood with his companions.

James McGill was responding primarily to financial prospects but also to the challenge to his manhood. He was a strong fellow and prided himself on his toughness. That first year he was one of the boys. Then he became a recognized Indian trader and led his own brigade, as a flotilla of canoes was called. But he still needed to show his men that he could hump a pack with the best of them and paddle as long as he demanded of others. Becoming a trader was no passport to an easy life. But always there was something more. Jean-Jacques Rousseau and William Wordsworth had not yet given words to the gospel of inspiring Nature, but McGill and

A Bark Canoe going down a rapid

Many of the first drawings of British Canada were made by officers in the armed forces. This one decorated a Canadian songbook published in 1823. Artist Lieut. G. Back, redrawn by Jane Kingsland.

his companions were nonetheless deeply aware of the captivating power of the land into which they had ventured. They had heard the silence of the forests, had come upon glades through which ran streams of limpid clarity, they had seen hills and great mountains majestic in their solitude, and inland seas stretching to limitless horizons; they had travelled all day under lofty skies and slept at night under canopies of stars and northern lights, and had awakened at dawn to the cry of the loon across a misty lake. Even though they returned from time to time or even permanently to the inhabited settlements, the wilderness experience never left them. They committed themselves to Canada and its ways of life because the country had laid its hold upon them.

The physical difficulties were not by any means the only ones to be overcome. The trader brought with him his "Indian goods" to be exchanged with the natives for furs, but that in itself was a complex undertaking. The main endeavour was to get the best pelts, that is, the winter ones. That meant the Indians must be persuaded to hunt and trap in winter, and they were no more disposed to undergo the hardships involved, if they could be avoided, than were their white partners. James learned from the start that to journey in the spring to Michilimackinac, barter there

with the Indians, collect the furs, and return after a summer stay
of only two to three weeks had become less and less rewarding.
The only way to gain a worthwhile return on the expenditure and
effort involved was to travel one year, pitch camp, and winter in
the wilderness, so as to have time to arrange matters with the Indians and barter at leisure, particularly in the spring, and then return to Montreal the following summer. When the British in the
early days of their regime mistakenly tried to forbid "wintering,"
the traders presented their practices as necessary for the sake of
"the poor Indian," but the pattern of trading was in fact necessary
for both partners:

It is well known that the Support of an Indian and his Family is his Fusee;
now if any Indian Family who perhaps Winters at the Distance of
five or six hundred miles from one of these established Forts, should by
any Misfortune either break his Fusee, or the least screw of his Lock be
out of order, or want Ammunition, where could that Indian Family be
supported from, or how get their Sustenance? They must either perish
with Hunger, or at least loose their Hunting that year ... Unless that Family is relieved by some Persons in the Fort giving them Credit, the ensu-
ing year they will not be able to return to their hunting Ground, and so be
lost for ever ... Without the Indians have Credit given them, 'tis impossible to carry on a Trade to Advantage. And when we are on the Spot to
winter with them, we always have an Opportunity of knowing their Dis-
positions, pressing them to exert their Diligence, and are ready in the
Spring to receive what is due.[3]

Those sentences are taken from a memorial dated from Montreal,
20 September 1766, the year of McGill's arrival in Canada, and addressed to Guy Carleton, the commander in chief, who was trying
to implement British control of the lands west of Montreal and of
the commerce with the Indians. The administrators had early instituted a system of allowing only licensed traders to operate, and
then only within the terms of their licences; but they too had to
learn that the fur trade could only operate in the patterns set by
climate and habitat.

But wintering certainly presented its own problems. A major
one was finding enough food for the long cold months. Provisions
could not be brought in quantity from Montreal since every
pound carried meant a pound less of trade goods. Corn could be

obtained from Indians but again at a cost of items which could have been exchanged for furs. Ice fishing was a slow, cold business and not dependable, game was often scarce and in the woods difficult to hunt. Rum for personal consumption had to be carefully rationed. Partly to ease the food supply and partly to broaden contact with Indians, the winterers scattered widely, alone or in pairs, so there was oppressive loneliness to be endured through the long months of dark winter nights. Then again the system of bartering was fraught with its own frustrations. The Indians could be induced to undertake the rigours of winter hunting and trapping only by the promise of trade goods – beads, knives, blankets, woollen and cotton goods, kettles, guns, powder and shot, and, of course, "fire water," the Indian name for West Indian rum. The usual practice was for the trader to contract with an Indian band to buy their furs at the end of the winter season when the more valuable winter coats could be had. Strangely, the skins regarded as the very best were those that had been worn for a season or two by the Indians; they trimmed the pelts roughly square, sewed them in panels with moose-leather thongs, and wore them with the fur inside. Their habit of rubbing bear grease on their bodies as a protection against cold, mosquitoes, and blackflies gave a shine to the pelt and also imparted a yellowish hue, so that a beaver robe two seasons or so old had a distinctive appearance and feel which the fur merchants came to prize very highly. Such skins were appropriately known as *castor gras*.

In order to attach a particular band to himself, a trader would give the Indians a small supply of goods and exchange promises with them to meet in the spring and barter more ample supplies for the band's winter catch. But if the band returning from its hunting grounds fell in with another trader and disposed of its catch to him, the first trader had no redress: the rule was that the last trader to have contact with the Indians had a right to acquire their skins. Hence the incentive to scatter widely and well away from other traders. In his first year, James McGill pushed on from Michilimackinac another two hundred miles to winter in Green Bay. Returns, of course, varied from season to season and from one locality to another, and so did prices. In 1775, when the Prairies and the Northwest were being more regularly visited, the prices established at Fort des Prairies in Saskatchewan were listed as follows: a "stroud" blanket (i.e., one of superior quality) was worth ten beaver skins, a white one, eight; an axe of one-pound weight, three; a half pint of gunpowder or ten balls, one, but the gun itself was worth twenty.[4] There was also much profit in the exchange of smaller articles: knives, beads, flints, steels, and awls. Rum would fetch two skins a bottle (it was normally much diluted) but the drink was generally reserved for gifting, an important element in the trading relationship. In the early years McGill had much to learn, especially with regard to native customs and etiquette.

That first winter, McGill was trading principally on behalf of his employer, William Grant, but in subsequent years he traded in his own interest. This meant that to acquire a sufficient stock in trade he had regularly to lay out the profits of previous journeys in the purchase of further supplies of trade goods in Montreal. After a year or two, he was able to arrange credit first in Montreal and then later in Quebec City. Once he was well established, he could make arrangements with the supply houses in London and purchase directly, and at a better price; but for that, in the early days at least, he had to be able to produce guarantors in Montreal or Quebec City. It all meant a careful campaign to gain credibility – in Montreal, in far-off London, at Michilimackinac, and at the very end of the line with the Indians at his bivouac in the Canadian winter wilderness. At every stage in that four-thousand-mile trade route, disaster could strike – a canoe upset in the rapids with a loss of goods, an accident in the woods or illness in the bivouac, a stormy winter and a poor catch for the Indians, failure of the Indians to keep the rendezvous, or their dealing with another trader; or once the pelts had reached Montreal for shipment to England, the ship might be lost at sea; and after all other perils had been surmounted, a change of fashions in London might bring a disastrous fall in prices. The fur trade was vulnerable at every point.

On the other hand, if all went well, profits could be substantial and considerable fortunes could be made. There was at this time no regular banking system and money values are very difficult to establish. The Spanish silver dollar was still a widely recognized standard, and Halifax merchants were willing to accept it as equal to five shillings in British money, so four dollars in Halifax equalled twenty shillings or one pound. But in London the exchange rate was five Spanish dollars to the British pound, so the

London pound was worth more than the Halifax pound. In the later years of the century pounds were also quoted in "New York currency." In Montreal it was generally the Halifax currency that was quoted but it is often difficult to be sure.[5] The relation of the pound to today's dollars is even more difficult to determine; one can only try to get a feel for what the figures meant to those who employed them. Beaver skins were worth roughly eight to the pound. Back in England at this time, Jane Austen ironically observed that a girl with a dowry of ten thousand pounds might reasonably expect to marry a baronet and so enter at least the lower levels of the aristocracy. At the other end of the scale, Oliver Goldsmith's impoverished "Vicar of Wakefield" was glad to accept a living that provided, in addition to house and glebe, only fifteen pounds a year on which to raise his numerous family; presumably their smallholding produced most of their food. One fur trader might set out with an outfit valued at £10,000 and return with a cargo of furs worth £15,000, so that the profit on one voyage alone might constitute a small fortune. Others might return with a meagre cargo and so gain little profit, or even sustain a loss on their venture. Benjamin and Joseph Frobisher made their first venture to the newly explored[6] Northwest in 1769, but on that trip they were robbed of their goods by hostile Indians and lost their investment. Simon McTavish, Alexander Mackenzie, and the Frobishers are examples of those who over the years fared well and became rich; so did James McGill, but it took him ten years of hard service, many of them passed wintering in the wilderness, before he could regard himself as moderately well established.

McGill began to trade seriously on his own behalf as early as 1767, that is, immediately after returning from his first venture into the Indian lands. He obtained a licence for two canoes and cargo worth four hundred pounds. In 1773, he shared a licence (it is not known what part he contributed – probably a third) with Benjamin Frobisher and Maurice Blondeau, for three guides and seventy-five men, and twelve canoes with a cargo of 100 gallons of rum and brandy, 24 kegs of wine (i.e., brandy), 64 kegs of gunpowder, 90 bags of ball and shot, 150 rifles, 150 bales of dry goods, 15 trunks of dry goods, 12 boxes of ironware, 12 "nests" of brass kettles, 100 packages of twist tobacco, 50 kegs of hogs' lard and tallow, and 60 kegs of pork. Twelve canoes was a large brigade and the total value of that cargo must have been around £6,000. In

1777, Jean Baptiste Adhemas was granted a licence for ninety-four men and ten canoes, which carried 440 gallons of liquor (mostly West Indian rum, but possibly some French brandy), 112 rifles, 3,700 pounds of gunpowder, 5,184 pounds of ball and shot, for a total value of £5,100. A few years later, a committee of merchants in Montreal, among whom was James McGill, reported to Governor Simcoe of Upper Canada that "the Indian country" probably owed them jointly as much as £300,000 sterling. Clearly, there were at any one time very large sums at risk, and while some venturers made substantial profits, there were often major losses.

As the trade expanded, a further development occurred in that when British military posts were established at such points as Michilimackinac and Detroit, a trader often settled there more or less permanently to act as a middleman between the Montreal merchants and the "pedlars," as they were sometimes called, who wintered among the Indians and conducted the actual barter. One such trader was John Askin, of whom we are going to hear a great deal. These middlemen became increasingly important in both the fur and the general trades.

From 1763, when the British war with the French ended, the traders from Montreal enjoyed twelve peaceful years in which they had to contend, apart from the usual vagaries of the trade, only with the controls emanating from Quebec City and with commercial competition from the English traders out of New York and Albany.[7] It was during this period of relative calm that James McGill became one of their number. The settlement of Upper Canada, as it was beginning to be called, along the shores of Lake Ontario past Kingston and York as far as Niagara and of New York Province past Buffalo to Detroit progressed rapidly and created a demand for household and farming goods, which could be paid for increasingly in grain and lumber as well as in furs. In addition, there were the military posts themselves to be supplied, which occasioned further traffic of great variety, and of course there was a garrison in Montreal to be maintained, and all these accounts were settled in good British sterling. These were all needs that the merchants of Montreal were well able and well placed to meet.

But in the early 1770s the brewing storm of the American War of Independence threatened to put an end to the period of peace. Perhaps it was no coincidence that it was in those years that McGill decided that he had risked life in the wilderness as a trader long enough and that he would use his gains to settle in Montreal and pursue his further career as a merchant. He reasoned that if there was to be war on the St Lawrence and the lakes between British and American forces, merchants in Montreal would no doubt be called upon to play a considerable role. It was an opportune moment to make the change from itinerant "pedlar" to the respectability of a merchant established in Montreal – if, that is, you were the kind of person who had the courage to risk everything you had gained so far on the uncertain fortunes of war. If the British won, loyalists were likely to be in favour and receive fresh opportunities, but if the Americans succeeded in exporting their revolution, those who had not supported their cause might well find they had lost their all. James McGill had not only the physical courage required for life in the wilderness but also had the merchant's brand of gambler's nerve. He decided to make the move.

However, before he could organize himself and his finances for his new career, he had unexpectedly to deal with a crisis from home. During James' fur-trading years, first his brother John and then his younger brother Andrew had followed him to Montreal, and both were seeking to establish themselves in the fur trade. John was two years younger than James but seems not to have had the same educational opportunities. He may have emigrated from Scotland at the same time as James and accompanied him to the Carolinas. If so, he stayed there when James left in 1766 to seek his fortunes in Canada and only followed him north four years later. Like James he went up country and wintered in the wilderness.[8] He shared some trading licences with James in 1773 but then he partnered a man called Paterson. We are left with the impression that John was following in a modest way in James' footsteps.[9] Over the years, he entered into a number of other ventures with various partners; in 1778, for example, a licence was granted to Thomas Frobisher and John McGill for twelve canoes, which was a sizeable venture, but we do not know how the outlay was divided between the two men.[10] John and the fur trader named Paterson subscribed in 1780 for two shares in the original North West Company, in which James and his partner had also taken two shares. John never entered into any other long-term partnership and never married. All this evidence suggests that the relationships between the elder brothers McGill were friendly but not close.

The third brother, however, had a more permanent relationship with James. The Carolinas do not figure in Andrew's story, and presumably he came out from Scotland straight to Montreal. He was eight years younger than James, had matriculated and spent some years in the University of Glasgow, and so was educationally more akin to the eldest brother. Arriving in Montreal a year or two after John, he went off after a few months to explore the commercial possibilities of Halifax. It is possible that he was sent by James to be his agent there, but if so the idea did not prove successful and he soon returned to Montreal to become a junior partner in the company James had set up. When that company went out of active business, James took Andrew into full partnership in the new James and Andrew McGill Company. Andrew also shared one or two minor business ventures with the middle brother. Even though there are indications that he played only a subordinate part in the McGill companies' business, Andrew's partnerships with James suggest that relations between the eldest and youngest brother were cordial, even if perhaps more like those of father and son.

These fraternal relationships set the scene for the incident of 1773–74. Back home in Scotland, James McGill II, the brothers' father, was continuing his social ascent by acquiring more property and borrowing funds to do so.[11] But in the way of real-estate dealers everywhere, he overreached himself and was not able to meet his liabilities. The father turned for help to his second son, John, who lent him four hundred pounds. Why did he turn to John? Why not to James? It raises the question whether James II and James III were not particularly close in their affection; it no doubt shamed the father to have to confess his difficulties to his sons, and perhaps it was easier to do this to the not-so-successful, more ordinary John than to the (perhaps in the father's eyes?) too headstrong, too independent James. Had James perhaps left Scotland in defiance of his father's wishes? In any case, when James heard of the matter he at once lent his father a further £1,150, which rescued him from his creditors, and then took over John's loan as well. He seems to have sent Andrew back to Glasgow to help sort out the father's affairs; the transactions ended with James II indebted to his eldest son to the tune of £1,500 and agreeing to pay £76 (five percent) yearly in interest. Was this the very situation that James II had foreseen and hoped to avoid? From James' point of view, his father's difficulties could not have arisen at a more unwelcome time, just when he was marshalling all his resources to make the move from trader to merchant. But his brothers were also in the midst of establishing themselves, and James recognized that it was for him to shoulder the responsibility. Probably it embarrassed him as much to make the loan as his father to receive it, and the businesslike interest arrangement was designed to help assuage the father's pride.[12]

During his arduous years as a voyageur, McGill formed friendships and acquaintances with many of the men he travelled and did business with. Some have left narratives of one sort or another relating their adventures. Unfortunately McGill himself was not among them. He was not much given to reminiscence and if sometimes in general conversation he recalled his early experiences, none of his anecdotes has survived. When in 1785 some of the traders in Montreal founded the Beaver Club, the qualification for which was to have wintered at least once in the wilderness. McGill joined readily and carefully preserved his gold medal of membership, struck with his date 1766 and the club's motto "Industry and Perseverance," illustrated by a beaver at work on a tree. The club's other motto, "Fortitude in Distress," was illustrated on the obverse of the medal by a canoe and its crew plunging manfully over a waterfall – a nice piece of sardonic humour.[13] At club reunions McGill sang the old boating songs with enthusiasm. After the meal, when the chairs were arranged two and two, as if in a canoe, he joined in vigorously, imitating the stroke of the paddlers in time with the music. He is also said to have been the one to propose that those who must return to their wives should leave at twelve midnight and the doors then be locked so that the songs, the reminiscences, and the rum might continue to flow uninterrupted. In his Montreal years, James McGill appears to exhibit such unvarying respectability that it is well to be reminded that for ten years (and probably earlier in the Carolinas) he had lived a very tough life and remained always a very strong, forceful personality. We can well believe that when he revelled, he revelled as forthrightly as he conducted all his other activities.

Both during and after his own pedlar activities, McGill formed partnerships with one or another of the fur traders to organize and finance particular ventures, or to provide services for traders acting on their own. Some of these expeditions he conducted him-

James McGill's Beaver Club Medal (front and back). The Beaver Club was founded in 1785 and McGill's year of qualification was 1766. Artist Jane Kingsland.

self, for others he provided the financial backing. One of the most colourful of the early traders was the American Peter Pond – soldier, seaman, trader, explorer, map maker, an impulsive, quick-tempered man, held responsible by his associates for at least two deaths in violent quarrels. In his autobiographical narrative he tells that in 1773 he was in Montreal procuring Indian goods, and, hearing that McGill and a trader named Isaac Todd were leading a brigade of canoes to the Great Lakes, he bargained with them for his passage with his goods, to Michilimackinac. It would have been interesting to know what McGill and Pond thought of each other after six or so weeks of close company. McGill would have admired Pond's courage and venturous character but not his impulsiveness and violence. McGill would often take risks, but they were always calculated risks, and he was from beginning to end very firmly a law-and-order man.

But he could appreciate characters very different from his own. The Isaac Todd just mentioned as McGill's trading partner in 1773 was an Irish merchant a year or two older than McGill who had settled in Montreal shortly after the British began to administer the city. He was established both in business and as a justice of the peace before McGill passed through the city for the first time in 1766. Todd was, in contrast to McGill, a naturally sociable, gregarious man and in later life was affectionately known as "By Jove Todd," since that was his favourite and much-used expression; he was also known for his readiness to reminisce about the early days of the fur trade and his experiences at Michilimackinac. He made numerous journeys to the fur traders' meeting place, but there is no evidence that he ever wintered over in the wilderness.[14] He was always more of a merchant than a pedlar. McGill and Todd came early to realize that they liked and trusted each other, and from 1769 on they collaborated in many ventures. Their first joint effort was undertaken that year in association with the Frobisher brothers – the same Frobisher expedition that was plundered by Indians, auguring poorly for any future activities. But a later, more formal Todd-McGill partnership was to prove very profitable, and for both men their friendship was to prove as significant as their business association.

Another long-time business associate whom McGill met during his fur-trader years was the John Askin mentioned earlier, also an Irishman. He had come to North America in 1758 and was a supplier to the British Army in Albany, New York, moving into the fur trade after the British acquired New France. Relations between white colonists and native populations were already deteriorating, and the British attempt to take over the former French military posts in Indian lands resulted in April 1763 in the uprising led by Chief Pontiac. This conflict spelled disaster for Askin's personal fortunes and it was 1771 before he was finally cleared of his debts. By that time he had moved to Michilimackinac and set up a general store to serve the numerous itinerant traders. Askin cultivated the friendship of the successive commandants at the British fort, and the favours he secured as a result enabled him to facilitate the business of fur-trading merchants. Todd and McGill were the most prominent of the many partnerships and individuals who found him useful as an agent in many ways. But Michilimackinac was a precarious place in which to do business, since war could at any time flare up again between the colonists and the Indians, or the threatening hostilities between the Thirteen Colonies and the British Government could turn to open warfare – all of which did in time come to pass, creating further long-standing difficulties for Askin and for his financial backers, including James McGill. John Askin had three children by an Indian companion and then nine more by a more regularly acquired wife. Since he very commendably held all his family in equal regard, he had many parental concerns and was to invoke the aid of his accommodating friend and business associate on several occasions.

What with his family and finances, he was to prove a troublesome friend, but he had great personal charm and always meant so well that his friends gave him a good deal of latitude. His outstanding virtue was that he had a great respect for correspondence, writing and receiving many letters which he carefully preserved, so that the Askin Papers are a mine of information about the fur trade and those who were active in it in the second half of the eighteenth century. McGill had to forgive Askin many debts; we are equally ready to forgive him all his shortcomings because he was such a prolific letter writer and took such good care of his correspondence.

After the British takeover of New France, traders bearing French names quickly began to appear in the lists of those licensed to trade with the Indians. Their expertise was essential to the continuance of the fur trade. Maurice Blondeau, Antoine Bourbonnois, Jean-Baptiste Rapin are typical of the many Canadiens active in the commerce during the decade when James McGill was traversing the forests, and he must have been familiar with many of them. He also of course mixed freely with the unnamed voyageurs who paddled his canoes and carried his packs. He learned their patois and became easy in their company. At least one of the Canadien traders became a member of the Beaver Club – Hippolyte Desrivières. He had a brother, Joseph-Amable Trottier dit Desrivières, to give him his full name, who was also a fur trader, and it is probable that McGill knew the brothers well. That acquaintance was to gain a particular significance later, when McGill decided to seek a more settled way of life.

All these fur-trading acquaintances and friendships made it easier for the young Scotsman, now aged thirty-one, to feel that Montreal had become truly his home, the place where he should put down roots. This lively, bustling little town, no longer the frontier settlement it had been for a century and a half but rather the embryo metropolis for the vast area reaching up to the Great Lakes and beyond – this little town he had come to regard as particularly his own. It was a loyalty that for the rest of his life was never to falter. It was also to serve as the basis for commitment to Canada, a country which was to undergo many changes in his lifetime, but which as the years passed meant for him more and more a land of opportunity and a truly civilized way of life.

3 Becoming a Montrealer, 1775–78

When McGill first saw Montreal in 1766, it was a small walled town of about five or six thousand inhabitants, apart from the British army garrison which increased its numbers by two or three hundred. The streets, he quickly discovered, were narrow and rather gloomy, muddy in spring and fall, in winter clogged with snow and ice, and in summer dusty and malodorous. Some of the houses were still built of wood, but after a great fire in 1721 rebuilding in stone had been strongly encouraged and stone houses were now in the majority. In these respects the city was not unlike the Glasgow he had left six or so years earlier. In the eyes of the young Scot, both when he first arrived and afterwards during subsequent visits, Montreal's European style gave it a homely, welcoming appearance. And small as it was, the town had already become a place of considerable commercial importance.

Sieur de Maisonneuve's decision in 1642 to establish a French colonial settlement on one of the islands in the Hochelaga archipelago of the St Lawrence River had been a shrewd one. The islands lie downstream from the Lachine Rapids, the first check on the river to seaborne shipping, and from the confluence of the St Lawrence and its major tributary, the Ottawa River. De Maisonneuve either knew or guessed that between them these two rivers opened up the whole of the western extent of the continent, including the huge Great Lakes basin, the Ohio River valley leading to the Mississippi and the South, and the vast prairies stretching

This drawing, published in 1762, shows Montreal as McGill would have first seen it, crossing from Longueuil in 1766. Artist Thomas Patten.

to the mountain range of the Rockies. The Hochelaga archipelago is in truth the inner gateway to North America; a settlement there could both command and exploit that entry.

De Maisonneuve decided to plant his new settlement in the shelter of the mountain rising on the largest of the islands, not far from where Jacques Cartier more than a century earlier had visited the Indian village of Hochelaga. Cartier had named the mountain Mont Royal, de Maisonneuve named his new settlement Ville Marie; but the dominating mountain soon passed its name to the settlement, which, apparently by a chance mapmaker's preference, received it in the form "Montreal" – without even the acute accent which orthographers have since added. The existence of a town with that name in France may have had some influence in the matter. But Montréal, Montreal, has been the city's name for three hundred and fifty years.

To establish the settlement on Montreal island was not only shrewd but also venturesome because the site lay dangerously open to Iroquois attacks. When Samuel de Champlain in the years between Cartier and de Maisonneuve made his pioneer explorations of the new continent, he found the Indian peoples already at war with one another. The groups he first encountered in regions around the mouth of the Saguenay and to the north and west of that area as far as the Ottawa River valley were the Montagnais and Algonquin, a loose confederation of farmers and seminomads. Their enemies were the more developed, more closely organized Six Nation Confederacy of the Iroquois. Champlain made the mistake of siding with one amalgamation against the other and the greater mistake of supporting the weaker side. Henceforth the fierce Iroquois were the implacable enemies of the French, and Montreal, if not actually in Iroquois territory, certainly in the no man's land between them and the Algonquin, was a post fraught with danger. Indian attacks were frequent: two rather more identifiable periods of hostilities in the first half of the seventeenth century have been called the first and second Indian Wars.

In the second half of the century the growing tensions between New France and the expanding English colonies to the south exacerbated the situation. The richer flow of Indian trade goods from the English sources of supply encouraged the Iroquois to ally themselves with the southerners and so to find new excuses to attack French settlements in the North. When France and England formally declared war and fought their quarrel to a conclusion, the city now officially at peace with the colonies to the south and with all the Indian tribes, entered for the first time into a period of comparative security.

It was during this interval of peace that the British traders, James McGill among them, came to Montreal and made it their point of departure for journeys into the Indian lands. These traders were a fluctuating population in Montreal because many of them came and went so frequently on their journeys "up country." But there was a small core of settled merchants and there were others sufficiently well known to one another to share common interests, so that it always was possible to gather a considerable number of signatures for their frequent petitions to the governor general and the executive council in Quebec City. James soon found that he was expected to have opinions and often solicited for support. These petitions generally asked that government restrictions on trade with the Indians be modified or lifted, and this was something to which James could readily subscribe. Another change the traders persisted in asking for was a legislative assembly so that the Province of Quebec might be governed by laws established by elected representatives, as had become the pattern in the English colonies to the south, and with that he went along with less conviction. In any case, the British had learned their lesson from the Thirteen Colonies and were slow to comply.

So even before James McGill had settled permanently in Montreal he had signed at least four petitions – one as early as 1767, another in 1770, and two more in 1774. In this way he was already taking part in the political life of the city and province. The petition of 1767, from traders assembled at Michilimackinac, stressed the importance of free trade with the Indians. Other signatories on that occasion were Isaac Todd, Alexander Henry, and Joseph-Amable Desrivières, all known to McGill as companions, friends, partners, or competitors. One of the petitions he signed in 1774 was composed by a committee of seven members, including McGill; it not only petitioned for a legislative assembly but also argued strongly for the institution of some form of English education in the province. Well aware of the value of his own education, McGill pushed for that clause strongly; throughout his subsequent career, this concern always won his interest and support.

When he decided to reside there permanently, Montreal had not changed greatly from his first impressions. It was still very much a frontier settlement. A mail for England was dispatched about once a month. It took three to four weeks to reach New York by way of the Richelieu, Champlain, and Hudson rivers; it was then forwarded by ship to England, and usually at least four months passed before an answer could be received. Incoming mail was put off the New York packet at Halifax; it came overland from Halifax to Montreal, this part of the journey alone taking nearly four weeks. Even to go to Quebec downriver could take anywhere from three days to three weeks depending upon the winds, or from several days to a week or more by the poorly maintained "Royal Road."[1] Once the river began to ice over, Montreal as a trading centre was isolated for four or five months.

But McGill had roughed it in the forests and camps for nine years, and to his eyes the city appeared cheerful, bustling, and attractive. The members of the British community were men of the style he was familiar with – typically Scots and Irish traders and merchants, English army officers, and a sprinkling of bureaucrats. He also knew many of the leading Canadiens; they had been his companions and associates in the fur trade. The working townspeople were the same kind of folk he had paddled canoes with, so that in the marketplace and the small stores where he shopped for daily necessities, or in the taverns where he dropped in for a drink or a meal, he could readily exchange greetings and news with his neighbours in either language, English or French. He had all the qualifications for becoming a good Montréalais.

McGill settled into the city in late 1774 or the early months of 1775. He was by now of sufficient substance to acquire a house, and he could begin to store goods in its cellars as he planned the pattern of trading on which he proposed to embark. He had already established himself in the good opinion of a London supply firm, Brickwood, Pattle and Company, and he had chosen the agents whom he would send out into the Indian trade. No doubt he was also hoping for commissions to supply goods for the British garrison in Montreal and its outposts at Oswegatchie, Kingston, Oswego, Detroit, and Michilimackinac. He passed an active summer and fall in 1775, organizing a brigade to go up country, receiving goods from England, and despatching furs, for summer was when the port of Montreal was busy; when the winter came and the port fell silent, that was the time for relaxation and further planning.

But he could not have started upon his new way of life with an undistracted mind, for it soon appeared that McGill's move to become a settled merchant had been a gamble that was likely to fail almost before it had begun. The English colonies had been in earlier years loud in their cries for Britain's help in relieving them of the competition and the hostility of the French, represented by the Canadiens of Quebec and Acadia and by the octopus spreading up the Mississippi from Louisiana, and particularly for protection from the depredations of the French navy and privateers. But once France had bowed out of North America by ceding Louisiana to Spain and New France to Britain, the colonists began to resent the taxes designed to recoup the costs of the war that had secured these benefits. The passing of the Quebec Act by the British Government in the spring of 1774, extending the boundary of that province to the northern bank of the Ohio River and the frontier with Louisiana,[2] did nothing to improve matters, for the new lines effectively barred Massachusetts, New York, and other English colonies from further westward expansion. The calling of the First Continental Congress in September of that year demonstrated the intention of the colonies to press their claims for independence. The original "No taxation without representation" soon became Patrick Henry's cry of "Liberty or Death." As the news and the rumours filtered through from London and Quebec City, from Boston, Albany, Philadelphia, and New York, James reflected ruefully that a time of civil strife and rebellion, possibly of outright war, was not a good time to launch a new business career. But there was nothing to do except steadily continue along his chosen path.

The Montreal merchants, of course, were greatly pleased with the new boundaries, for they removed many of the irritating restrictions on their fur-trading activities. The Canadiens, for their part, saw it as merely restoring the situation to the *de facto* state of affairs that had existed before the British came interfering; they had always felt that their writ ran as far as the Mississippi, their trunk line of communication with their compatriots in Louisiana. The Montreal merchants, however, found there was much else in the new act that was not at all to their liking. They resented the fact that it gave legitimacy to the French language and that it restored the French legal system in civil cases; a great many of the merchants signed a protest, saying that by this provision historic British rights, such as the option of trial by a jury of one's peers, had been set aside, and that even in criminal cases, where British law had been maintained, the protection of the Habeas Corpus Act had been abrogated.[3] In addition, of course, the merchants particularly deplored the omission from the legislation of the right to elect a provincial assembly. In their view these elements of the Quebec Act were simply designed to win favour with the Canadiens and to ensure their loyalty to the British Crown in any coming conflict with the English colonists to the south and were not only unnecessary but would positively encourage a nascent Canadien nationalism.

It is highly significant that James McGill did not sign the petition; the protest had been strongly promoted among the merchants and his failure to sign can hardly have been accidental. It suggests that even at this early stage in his career as a merchant, he shared Governor General Carleton's view that the prosperity of the Province of Quebec required cooperation with the Canadiens as a foundation element in its constitution; he recognized that they must be given a full partnership in the administration of the province and must be allowed to retain their religion, their language, and, at least in civil affairs, their laws. At this stage, James was no more enamoured of the idea of an elected Quebec legislative assembly than Carleton himself; he probably shared the fairly widespread eighteenth-century prejudice against "mob rule." Later, he was to come round to the view that reintroducing French law in civil affairs was a good thing in itself but had created such legal confusion in the province that a legislative assembly, able to sort out the difficulties, was indispensable. But in 1775 he was content to withhold his signature from the petition protesting the contentious act. It was well known that the troublesome parts of the legislation had been largely shaped by Guy Carleton,[4] who strongly resented the petition and, it was said, never forgave the signatories. It probably did James no harm in later years that he had not been among them, even though he was to sign several other petitions, some of which pressed the cause of representative government very hard. The change of heart occurred after he had had personal experience of the confusion that could arise in a country where two different legal systems were concurrently in use.

But it was within the city itself that James had to learn to pick his way very carefully between conflicting interests, loyalties, and downright plottings. It must be remembered that it was still only a decade and a half since Montreal had come under British control. Immediately after the conquest the authorities had imposed military rule, which included billeting the new garrison in the houses of the inhabitants, and this, apart from all else, was a source of much irritation to the original French-speaking citizens. But the local commander, General Murray, appears to have tried hard to keep his men in check and to have done his best to correct any abuses, and after a while the Canadiens became more trusting of the good intentions of their new masters. A compromise attitude of live and let live seems to have developed between the citizens and the army, but a further problem was created by attempts to supplement military rule with the rudiments of a civil regime, and this created divisions within the English-speaking community. James found that both sides were more than ready to tell him their version of events.

As early as 1764 justices of the peace were appointed and given limited powers of summary jurisdiction; provision was also made for a grand jury, to sift cases and decide their disposal, and for a

Court of King's Bench. The great difficulty, however, was to procure suitable personnel to operate the system. At this time Catholics were debarred in England from holding office under the British Crown, and the same rule was applied in Canada, rendering the major part of the population ineligible for appointment. The small numbers of Protestants who were available consisted mostly of discharged soldiers, many of them quite uneducated, and the "British" merchants. But these last were a mixed bunch, many of them unscrupulous traders intent only on getting rich quickly. Murray had invited merchants from New York and Albany to come help victual the garrison in Montreal, and those who had responded were the more adventurous and some, no doubt, the less trustworthy of their kind; he soon formed a poor opinion of them. His successor quickly came to share this view and roundly called the merchant "rascals": on 28 March 1770 Carleton reported to Lord Hillsborough, secretary for the Colonies:

Your Lordship has already been informed that the Protestants who have settled, or rather sojourned here since the conquest, are composed only of Traders, disbanded soldiers and officers, the latter one or two excepted, below the Rank of Captain; of those in the Commission of the Peace, such as prospered in business, could not give up their time to sit as Judges; and when several from accidents and ill-judged undertakings became Bankrupt, they naturally sought to repair their broken fortunes at the expense of the People; hence a variety of schemes to increase their own business and their own emoluments.[5]

It is not surprising, then, that men like Isaac Todd or James McGill were readily welcomed as candidates, since in character and education they stood above many of their fellows. In his next letter to Hillsborough, dated a month later, Carleton himself acknowledged grudgingly that "there are worthy men in the commission of the peace." Todd had been a magistrate since 1765; McGill was appointed to the commission in 1776.

Everyone agreed that those parts of the Quebec Act of 1774 that sought to deal with these legal and social problems were therefore very much needed, but not every one agreed with the solutions the act instituted. It confirmed the right of the Canadiens to practise their own religion and to conduct their civil affairs by the customs of their own French law, and it amended the oath of allegiance to the British Crown in such a way that Catholics could henceforth exercise civic rights and be eligible to serve in public offices. Canadiens could sit on grand juries, practise in courts of law, or be appointed magistrates. James McGill could only approve these developments warmly, and his confidence in the general administration of the province was that much strengthened. But the continued rule of the city by appointed magistrates rather than by elected aldermen, and above all the presence of an army continuing to exercise a degree of military rule, could not make for peaceful cooperation in the city. There was considerable tension between the military and the magistrates, and of course among the Canadiens a certain amount of resentment towards both. There were not many in the city who could move as easily as James McGill, purveyor to the army and himself a magistrate, from one British group to the other, and, as a former "pedlar" fur trader, still meet with acceptance among the Canadiens also.

So the reforms of 1774 could not immediately right all wrongs, and there were many resentments still left burning, as one incident arising from the early days of the magistracy illustrates. There were many in the officers' mess, in the merchants' hotel bars, even in the corner taverns, who were anxious to tell McGill the "truth" of the affair. A householder, a Canadien, let rooms to a magistrate under the impression that this removed him from the list of those liable to have soldiers billeted upon them. But the army required him also to find a room for a junior officer, Captain Payne. The landlord thereupon appealed to another magistrate, Thomas Walker, who upheld the privileges of the magistracy and ordered Payne to vacate the room. Payne refused and was committed to jail for contempt of court.

This Thomas Walker was an Englishman who had emigrated to Boston and moved on to Montreal in 1760, immediately after the Conquest. He openly professed strong democratic ideas and, said the gossips on the one side, "in many ways showed that he was no friend of the Military ... He was a bold, aggressive man, who set himself up as an agent of the people, [and] opposed the actions of General Murray in every way."[6] Nevertheless, in 1764 Murray, short of candidates, had had little choice but to appoint him a justice of the peace, and so it happened that he sat in the case concerning Captain Payne. The army officers construed his actions on that occasion in siding with his fellow magistrate and jailing an officer for contempt as another provocative instance of his previous unfriendly attitude to the military. Two days after the judgment, armed men in disguise broke into Walker's rooms as he and his family were at dinner, allowed the other members of the family to escape, and proceeded to rough Walker up severely, while uttering fearful curses and violent death threats, but in fact doing no more permanent damage than cutting off a part of one ear. The attackers were supposed to be genuine desperadoes, but to the magistrates it looked very like a piece of drunken buffoonery by army bullies thinking to intimidate the civilian authorities.

Six men, most of them young officers, were charged with committing this outrage and were hauled from their beds in the middle of the night and taken off to Quebec. Walker insisted on a jury trial (this was before Catholics were given the exercise of civil rights) but then refused to travel to give testimony in Quebec City or even in Trois Rivières, where a sufficient number of Protestants could have been mustered. The trial was ultimately held in Montreal on 1 July 1765 and all the accused were acquitted. Even then the matter was not ended; it dragged on into the following year before finally petering out for lack of evidence. But it was still a frequent topic of conversation when McGill returned to the city on his biennial visits, and he found it best to listen sympathetically to all parties and say little. A wise merchant does not alienate potential customers.

McGill did not himself warm to Walker, but in the close social circles of Montreal he was a difficult fellow to ignore. He claimed to have influence in government circles and to have been instrumental in getting Murray recalled to England. His successor, Guy Carleton, found the testy magistrate as much trouble as had his predecessor. As the tension between the American colonists and the British government increased, so Walker's support for the colonists' claims to independence became more open and more partisan. He had gathered a small radical group who shared his ideas, and in April 1775 he organized a meeting of American sympathizers in a Montreal coffee shop, where he openly advocated sending Quebec delegates to the next Continental Congress. McGill was prudently absent but his friend Isaac Todd was persuaded to be one of the committee named to compose the communication to the Americans. Rumours began to circulate that Walker had communicated military intelligence to Benedict Arnold, at the time a Connecticut militia captain, and to Ethan Allen, the commander of the Vermont irregulars known as the Green Mountain Boys. In June McGill heard that he was active in the areas of Repentigny and Chambly, where he was purchasing corn from the farmers and at the same time promising money, arms, and ammunition to those who would side with the Americans. So in the early months of the fateful year, while some members of the English-speaking community had stoutly declared themselves for the king, there were others, like Walker, who publicly or overtly supported the aims of the colonists – and there were many more who sat on the fence, waiting for the fighting to be over, when they would declare themselves for the victors. All that summer Montreal was an uneasy, anxious, and divided community, and James McGill found himself in the midst of competing factions.

From the loyalists' point of view the news from the South during those months was not reassuring. In April 1775 the first shots of the conflict were fired at Lexington and Concord on the approaches to Boston, and later that month British forces won a costly victory in a full-scale battle at Bunker Hill. Then in May, the news reached Montreal that the Green Mountain Boys, led by Ethan Allen with support from Benedict Arnold, had actually captured the forts of Ticonderoga and Crown Point, the two supposed "strong" holds on the old Hudson-Lake Champlain-Richelieu route from New York.

On the island of Montreal there was much apprehension and considerable confusion. Guy Carleton was himself in the city trying to rally a defence force to oppose the expected attack on the St Lawrence valley at either or both of its major bastions, Montreal and Quebec City. He appealed to the seigneurs of the estates in the area, on and off the island, to call up their tenantry to serve in the militia alongside the two or three hundred troops of the Montreal garrison. But the tenants told their seigneurs that their feudal obligations of military service had ended when the French Crown was superseded by the British. When the population of Montreal, including the British merchants, was assembled in the Champs de Mars and the men present were ordered to join the armed forces quartered in the barracks, some responded but many more, those favourable to the Americans and those indifferent to either side, turned away and ignored the call to arms.

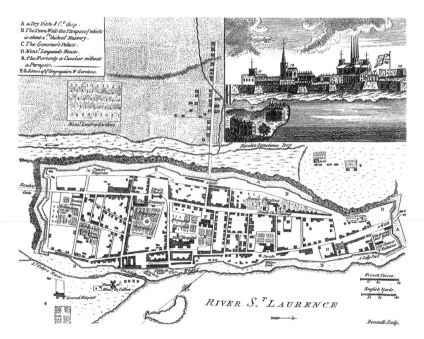

A Plan and View of the Town and Fortifications of Montreal in Canada. Engraving from the *Grand Magazine*, 1760.

The year 1775 was, then, a time when a man had to declare himself, and James McGill weighed his previous reasoning carefully before making his decision. Should peace prevail and the fur trade be left undisturbed, he could of course continue to engage in it, but if the war dragged on, the Indian lands and the Indian trade would almost certainly be dangerously unsettled for an undetermined period. But in that circumstance, the British forces would certainly need supplies, and those merchants who, like James, were already familiar with the country, and with that kind of commission, would be in a position of strong advantage. Further, if the British succeeded in suppressing the rebellion, he would be in favour with the ruling powers; but in the unlikely event that the colonists would not only win their freedom but would export their revolution to Canada, he would be in a most unfavourable situation. He had already heard stories of attacks upon loyalists and the looting of their properties. There were risks to be run, whether the outcome proved to be peace or war. He based his own conclusion partly on personal inclinations of sentiment and loyalty, but also on what he believed were sound business considerations: a merchant's first duty was to promote his business as forthrightly as political and other circumstances would allow. That was his necessary contribution to his community, as well as in his own self-interest. He decided to remain with his determination to support the British government.

Meanwhile, the American general Montgomery, having advanced up the Richelieu, was preparing to besiege St John's. With him were Ethan Allen and his Green Mountain Boys. To give Allen and his men something to do, Montgomery sent him on to Longueuil to keep watch on Montreal and prevent a counterattack from the city. But at La Prairie Allen met with Colonel Brown, another commander of American irregulars, and the two hatched a scheme to capture Montreal while Montgomery was still preoccupied with St John's, which was holding out with great determination. The plan was very simple. Brown would cross the river with the larger force and land west of the city; Allen and his men would cross to Longue Pointe east of the city; then on a signal given by Brown, they would attack simultaneously and rush the unprepared defences of Montreal from two sides. They were further encouraged in their scheme by the news that the British at Fort Chambly had surrendered with hardly a shot fired. On the night of 24 September Allen set off and, after much trouble with river currents, landed his small force on Montreal Island by early morning. The inhabitants of Longue Pointe showed no great friendliness to the invaders, nor particular animosity, but one farmer slipped away into the city with the news of their arrival. Allen waited for Brown's signal, but none came: he and his men were now isolated in a dangerous position. Once alerted, Carleton immediately sent Major John Campbell with a mixed force, regulars and militia, to contain the threatened attack.[7] Among the militiamen were two new lieutenants, James McGill and Isaac Todd. Probably James had played no small part in persuading Isaac to change his mind; they must have held many long and anxious discussions. Campbell made his way to the east and engaged the invaders. Ethan Allen made a show of resistance, but quickly surrendered. He was taken prisoner and jailed in the hold of one of the armed sloops in Montreal harbour, where he was speedily joined by Thomas Walker, of whose disloyalty and treasonable activity Carleton had by now had more than enough.

This small victory heartened the defenders of Montreal and encouraged the merchants who were loyal to the Crown to sign a manifesto, which was displayed prominently in Montreal and published in the Quebec *Gazette* – there was as yet no newspaper published in Montreal. It was subscribed on 2 October 1775 by some sixty-seven British merchants and the list of names included those of James McGill and Isaac Todd. The text of the manifesto ran as follows:

Whereas the publick peace and tranquility as well as the Trade and Commerce of this Province has for some time past been greatly interrupted and almost wholly impeded by a set of Invaders who have come into the Province, in a hostile manner and taken up Arms against and attacked His Majesty's Troops, and the peaceable Inhabitants of this Province, whereby their Lives and Properties have been exposed to the greatest danger, We the Subscribers, his Majesty's faithful Subjects, being convinced that the most effectual means to prevent their wicked designs will be to promote harmony and unanimity among ourselves, Do unanimously resolve and solemnly promise and agree to and with each other respectively that we will, to the utmost of our Power, oppose their Intentions, and defend our Lives and Properties against all such Invaders, their Adherents, Associates and Abettors, and that we will make the cause of each of us the General Cause of the whole.[8]

This declaration of support persuaded Carleton to adopt a more offensive plan. He loaded his men, now numbering with the militia volunteers seven or eight hundred, into a flotilla of thirty-five or forty boats to cross to Longueuil and from there march to the relief of St John's, which was maintaining its heroic defence. Once again Todd and McGill were enlisted with the militia. But yet another American commander had seized the strong point at Longueuil and strengthened it with several field guns taken from Chambly. Loaded with grapeshot and fired into the densely packed boats, they created fearful damage. When the canons were supported by sustained rifle fire, Carleton was forced to order the retreat. He lost forty to fifty men and had about the same number wounded; fortunately both Todd and McGill escaped unharmed. The news of the defeat spread widely and was quickly followed by the capitulation of St John's.[9] Montgomery then began to move towards Montreal. Carleton, realizing that the surrender of the city was inevitable, boarded his sloops, taking with him some 150 of the regular army and his two important prisoners, Allen and Walker, and set off down river, leaving the city to make its own terms with the advancing Americans.

But the fates, or at least the winds, were against him. At Lavaltrie, twelve miles short of Sorel, the fleet was held captive for two days by contrary winds. The Americans soon arrived on shore and called on Carleton to surrender. Leaving behind his ships and his forces, but not his prisoner Ethan Allen, the British commander and a few close associates took to a barge and in the night crept past the batteries the Americans were busy erecting. The stranded ships quickly surrendered, but Carleton succeeded in reaching Quebec City.

So Ethan Allen went off to close confinement,[10] while Thomas Walker returned triumphantly to Montreal to play host to his victorious American friends. On 13 November 1775, the Congress troops of the Continental Congress, many of then incongruously wearing the scarlet uniforms of the British forces found in the stores of Fort Chambly and St John's, entered the city by the Recollet Gate[11] on the west and, having received the keys to the storehouses of the city, marched proudly along Notre Dame Street to the barracks facing the Champs de Mars. The *New England Chronicle* was quick to spread the news: "Dispatches for His Excellency, General Washington. News of Montreal's quiet submission of that city to the victorious arms of the United Colonies of America."[12]

With his usual taciturnity, James McGill left no record of his activities during these tumultuous days. But it is known that he and his friend Isaac Todd accepted commissions in Carleton's militia, and that he had openly declared for the king. Having bound himself with his neighbours to oppose the intentions of the enemy "to the utmost of our Power" and to stand together "to defend our Lives and Properties," McGill shared fully in Montreal's experience of war. He was to have a long and distinguished career in the militia, a career that began in the stirring events of a city fighting back against attack.

That winter McGill shared the bitterness of living under the heavy hand of an occupying army, for when Carleton left, McGill did not take the opportunity, as did some, to slip away and make for safer areas. Montgomery established himself first in the Recollet suburb outside the western wall of the city, where twelve citizens, six francophone and six anglophone, were deputed to meet with him to discuss the terms of the surrender. One of those twelve was James McGill.[13] The Americans made the point that they came not as a conquering or invading force but as a liberating army poised to bring freedom and democracy to their enslaved brothers, whether English- or French-speaking. The Montrealers put forward their terms for a peaceful, unresisting surrender, though they knew full well they did not have the power to resist. Their main points were that the religious orders should enjoy their rights and properties; French and English (in effect, Catholics and Protestants) should be allowed the full exercise of their religion; trade in the upper parts of the province, the interior, and beyond the seas should flow uninterrupted; passports should be issued to those wanting to travel on legitimate business; no citizens should be forced to bear arms against the mother country and prisoners of war should be released; the courts of justice should be reestablished and the judges elected by the people; the American commander should make provision for the peace of the city; and the citizens should not be forced to take in American soldiers billeted upon them. Montgomery accepted most of these "demands" but said he could not give any undertakings concerning trade with the British, and with that understanding he marched his men into the city.

These terms of surrender are revealing, for they reflect the interests of the two groups representing the city. Both Canadiens and British wanted life to go on very much as it had in the past: the only democratic innovation was that the magistrates in future should be elected, not appointed. But whereas the Canadiens made a point of stressing freedom of religion, the British were anxious to preserve freedom of trade – the freedom of merchants to trade into the Indian lands, to pass their furs to British and European markets, and to continue their commercial relationships with the London houses. These last concerns touched James McGill so closely that he certainly would have had a voice in the framing of the commercial articles of the agreement. He must have known that in the present confused situation, no one on either side of the conflict could guarantee the smooth flow of trade, but there was no harm in getting what was vitally important for all parties clearly stated: Montreal could survive only as a trading city. The choice of McGill as a member of the delegation indicates that he was gaining stature in the town; he had shown himself valiant in the defence of the city and now he was being watchful of the best interests of all its citizens, Canadien and British alike.

During the winter of 1775–76 the American forces occupied Montreal. A few of the British community, Walker among them, rejoiced in the new order; a greater number tolerated it and were prepared to see how things worked out; others, like McGill, increasingly resented it and waited grimly for the British relief they confidently expected. The first news was that the Americans were mounting an attack on Quebec, the next that the Americans had launched a courageous assault, which had been as courageously repulsed; then came word that the attackers had settled down to besiege the city. Everyone waited to see if cold and hunger would triumph where gallantry had failed. McGill reflected that if Quebec fell, British rule in Canada was likely to end and all the former North American possessions would be joined in a new independent confederation, in which case his own future and the commercial future of the province would be uncertain to say the least. If, on the other hand, Quebec held out and the British navy arrived with reinforcements in the spring, Canada would be saved and the tide of war would probably recede to the south. Life and trade, it could be hoped, would return to normal.

As the weeks passed into months, James McGill had plenty of opportunity to observe with considerable satisfaction the deteriorating relations between the Americans and the people of the city. Montgomery was succeeded as American commander by a stiff-necked New England Puritan named Wooster. He committed the incredible blunder of ordering the "mass houses," as he called Catholic churches, to be locked shut on Christmas Eve. He also tried to put a stop to Montreal's Indian trade on the grounds that it was aiding the Union's enemies. In this way he succeeded in alienating the sympathies of Canadien and British alike. Wooster was soon replaced by Benedict Arnold, the hero of the gruelling march on Quebec City by way of the Kennebec and Chaudière rivers. But the damage had been done.

Another major problem was simply financial. The surrounding parishes could feed the city and the occupying forces: the difficulty was how to arrange payment. Coins of any denomination were in short supply; British paper, which had circulated none too freely, was now gone and no one trusted the new American so-called "Continental" bills. When the Congress in Philadelphia sent three commissioners to Montreal to repair Wooster's blunders by explaining the ideals of republicanism and the joys of independence to the Quebec farmers and the Montreal bourgeoisie, they themselves ran straightway into this problem of cash. They wrote back to Philadelphia: "It is impossible to give you a just idea of the lowness of continental credit here, from the want of hard money and the prejudice it is to our affairs. Not the most trifling service can be purchased without an appearance of instant pay in silver or gold. The express [letter] we sent from St John's [to Montreal] to inform the general of our arrival here, and to request carriages for La Prairie had to wait at the ferry [here in St John's] till a friend, passing, changed a dollar for us into silver."[14]

The same "friend" also had to pay for the hire of carriages or the commissioners would never have arrived in Montreal. But it was not only the commissioners who were in difficulty; it was the Americans generally, from the commander down to the enlisted men. The army could commandeer food, clothing, and other articles and pay farmers and storekeepers in Continental paper, but especially to the Québécois that looked very much like outright theft. Individual soldiers found their pay worthless in the markets and the local inhabitants less and less friendly. James McGill hoarded his own cash and goods while he watched the American situation deteriorate. At least once his house was visited by the army commissariat – or raided by lawless looters; McGill did not draw much of a distinction – and he lost fourteen puncheons of West Indian rum that he had laid in for John Askin. Otherwise he seems to have been unmolested, for although he made no attempt to hide his opinions, he took no overt action against the invaders. His house served on at least one occasion as a gathering place for those still loyal to the British cause. Wooster required militia officers to surrender their commissions to him and a number of them met in McGill's home to consider their response; apparently they agreed on at least the appearance of compliance, but some managed secretly to retain their warrants.[15]

In contrast, Magistrate Walker moved into the house built by Baron Bécancour on the west side of the Château de Ramezay, the American commander's headquarters. Here he played host to the commissioners, who were a very distinguished trio: Benjamin Franklin, the philosopher and wise man of the revolutionary movement, Samuel Chase of Maryland, distinguished jurist and member of the Congress, and Charles Caroll, one of the wealthiest men in the colonies, a Catholic by religion and completely bilingual in French. With Caroll was his brother John, a former Jesuit (the Society of Jesus was at that time suppressed) who was later to become the first archbishop of Baltimore. But able and persuasive as these four were, they discovered that the Canadian clergy were deeply suspicious of all things republican – perhaps they could already scent the rationalism and atheism of the coming French Revolution and saw the British Crown as a preferable defence. Without the good will of the clergy, Franklin's philosophy and the Caroll brothers' piety could do nothing. The commissioners had also brought with them a French printer named Fleury Mesplet. His task was to produce pamphlets to help spread republican ideas among the general population. He was installed in the basement of the château and soon proved himself useful by establishing Montreal's first newspaper, *La Gazette Littéraire*. It appeared once a week, in French; later it became bilingual. Now called *The Gazette* and printed in English only, it is still one of Canada's major daily publications. But Mesplet's revolutionary pamphlets met with little success, and to secure an income he was soon busy printing booklets of Catholic piety.

The end came in May 1776 with the report of the arrival of a British fleet in the St Lawrence, the subsequent news of the relief of Quebec City, and the withdrawal of the Americans. The retreat was not wholly peaceful. There was a lively skirmish at Les Cèdres on the St Lawrence, where a small British detachment from Oswegatchie bluffed a much larger American force into surrender; a scrambling battle at Trois Rivières where the Americans largely defeated themselves, lost in woods and swamps; and "a humiliated, demoralizing retreat" up the Richelieu "marked by a long line of graves."[16] Carleton did not pursue them vigorously; he just made sure they left Canadian soil. He even gave stragglers a clean shirt and a little money to help them reach their homes, sadder and wiser men. And, of course, to share the tale of their disastrous experiences with their neighbours. It was both a humane gesture and a wise policy.

Franklin and his fellow commissioners had long since realized that it was time for them to go. They left Montreal on 17 May, with Mrs Walker in their party. Walker joined them later, and husband

and wife were left in Albany, while the commissioners continued on to report their unhappy failure in Philadelphia.[17]

So the Americans were gone. James McGill's gamble had so far proved successful and he could cautiously resume his career. Already he had three major projects in view for this year 1776. First, he needed to send an agent up to Michilimackinac with what Indian goods he still had in store to renew contact and good will with the Indian tribes; they would be feeling the pinch very acutely. Equally important was his expectation that a load of furs from last year's trading would be waiting for his agent and needed to be brought down that summer. The sooner they could be shipped off to the London market, the sooner would his credit be restored in the supply houses – they too must have had some anxious hours during the past winter. He had already prepared the long list of goods that he needed to import for the next season's trading.

His second project was to consolidate further his position as fur trader and general merchant by strengthening his standing in the merchant community. To do this he sought to ally himself with another merchant in a long-term partnership where the good reputation and the financial resources of each partner would support those of the other. It is perhaps a little surprising that the chosen collaborator should be Isaac Todd, given that Todd tended initially to favour American rather than British interests and was so unlike McGill by way of personality. In business affairs, he was more inclined to remain with the fur trade and participate in the opening up of the Northwest, whereas McGill was ready to welcome the expansion of general trade around the Great Lakes. But these differences could prove to be the strength of the partnership. It was true that Todd's commercial record thus far had not been overly successful. He had settled in Montreal early in 1765. In a fire on 18 May of that year he had lost goods that no doubt cost him a good deal more than the £150 he claimed in insurance. In 1768 he again suffered a substantial loss when two of his hired traders were killed by hostile Indians. The next year he and McGill both invested in Benjamin and Joseph Frobisher's first venture to the Northwest – the expedition plundered by Indians at Rainy Lake. All four partners lost their investment, Todd to the tune of nine hundred pounds. In early 1773 he lost two more men "starved or killed" near Grand Portage, at the far end of Lake Superior.

But there was a great deal to be said to balance the scale. Although he had suffered trading reverses, Todd had always bounced back. Later in 1773, for example, he had joined with McGill to take several canoes (and, it will be recalled, Peter Pond as passenger) very successfully up to Michilimackinac. But it was in 1774 that he achieved his best business *coup*: he was appointed agent in Montreal for the important American firm of Phyn, Ellice and Company of Schenectady, New York. He gave the Americans advice on how to circumvent new British taxes on their profitable trade supplying Montreal with West Indian rum; they in return gave him foreknowledge of the arrival date of American shipments of that vital commodity. This kind of insider knowledge could prove invaluable to the projected partnership. Todd was in fact one of those men who knew everybody and knew what was afoot – in Montreal, in Quebec City, in Albany, in New York, in the fur trade generally.[18] The two men, Todd and McGill, had worked together, travelled arduously together, shared danger together, trusted one another, and, perhaps most importantly, complemented each other. Todd, McGill and Co. was in fact to prove a durable partnership. Todd's name went first because he was the older man, more experienced and better known; but as the years passed, more and more often McGill's was the deciding voice. One letter addressed to the company referred to "Mr McGill your doyen," and in letters to Todd, James wrote almost as if Isaac were a sleeping partner, needing to be informed of deals in which he himself had played no part. But it was on both sides a very comfortable relationship. A passage from a letter John Askin wrote to Isaac Todd nearly forty years after the Todd-McGill partnership first began perfectly sums up their relationship: "Nothing would be a greater loss to Mr McGill than [that] of your Society; he loves you as a brother, and you always brought home dayly news, interesting and amusing, which he otherwise could not have had; his natural turn being not to mix, but with a few chosen friends."[19]

Towards the end of this decisive period, when the Americans were gone and the port was shut down for the winter, McGill had time and leisure to attend to his third and even more important project. On the corner of Rue St François and Rue de l'hôpital stood a well-built house, formerly the property of McGill's fur-trading companion Joseph-Amable Trottier dit Desrivières. Joseph had died four years earlier but his widow still lived in the house and on the ground floor she kept a small store. James began to make cautious enquiries about her. He learned that she was still comparatively young – in fact, twenty-nine, two years younger than he was. Her maiden name was Guillimin, and as a magistrate McGill had come to know her father, Guillaume. He had been one of the first Canadiens to learn his law in New France, having been articled to the then attorney general. He had served in several capacities as a judge under the French regime and was one of the few Canadiens who had managed to continue in his profession under British rule. As a Catholic could not, of course, continue in the judiciary, but he was licensed by the British to practise as a lawyer in the Court of Common Pleas and when after 1766 a wider emancipation was granted to Catholics, he along with three others obtained the right to practise in all the courts. No doubt these developments represented a decline from his former social position and probably income, but he remained a much respected person. He had, in fact, pioneered in Montreal that success in the learned professions which so many Canadiens were to achieve in later years.[20]

Charlotte Guillimin, therefore, came of good stock and James McGill could observe in his visits to her store that she was a comely young woman who comported herself in accordance with her upbringing. He knew that she had known much sadness. Her two little daughters had both succumbed to childhood diseases; widowed at age twenty-five, she had been left to bring up her two boys, François, now aged twelve, and Hippolyte, aged seven. James could respect a woman who had faced adversity with courage and determination; her little store had helped to preserve a home for herself and her sons. What James had seen of the boys pleased him; they had been *bien élevés*. Hippolyte was named after his uncle, Hippolyte Desrivières, another of McGill's fur-trading companions. Altogether, he already knew a good deal about the Desrivières family and believed that he could fit into its relationships very comfortably. Most importantly he was favourably impressed with the young woman herself. Until now he had led an independent but also lonely life. A pleasing young wife presiding over his home would complete his picture of himself as a respectable and responsible citizen.

Of course, Charlotte was a Catholic and he by upbringing a Presbyterian, so they could not be married in her church, but they could be married by the minister of the Protestant congregation, the Reverend David Delisle, a French-speaking Swiss. Charlotte, whose English at this stage was not very proficient, could thus have most of her service in French and continue after the wedding in her church and James in his. He himself was broad minded in religious matters and he knew that most Catholics would not balk at so promising a union, even if their church could not officially recognize it. Through his marriage James McGill would forge further valuable alliances with the Canadien community; for her part, Charlotte was no longer a struggling widow, but a young matron supported by a rising merchant. He proposed and she accepted; they were married on 2 December 1776. Among the witnesses were her brother Hippolyte and his brother John; Andrew was probably absent in Halifax at this time.

The union of James and Charlotte was to prove very comfortable and continued happily into old age. At the beginning it may well have been a union of the head rather than the heart; for example, the two parties entered into a marriage contract that declared them to be separate as to property, an unusual feature in those days. Undoubtedly the thinking was that if McGill failed in business (a not infrequent event in the merchant community), his wife at least would not lose her own property to his debts. McGill was careful to state that, in the event of his death, Charlotte's marriage portion would be "sixteen thousand shillings of this province," that is, eight hundred pounds – not as large a sum as would have been appropriate in later life, but as much as McGill could reasonably promise at that time. All his life James treated "Mrs McGill" with great respect and there is little doubt that over the years a steady affection grew between them.

Early in 1777, McGill was able to give Charlotte something that surely pleased her greatly. The house next to the Château de Ramezay was one of the most desirable residences in the city. It fronted on Rue Notre Dame and had been the property of the Baron de Bécancour during the last years of the French period. It was the same house in which Thomas Walker had so ostentatiously entertained the American envoys from Philadelphia, and it had come on to the market soon after the Walkers' hasty departure. James McGill bought it and there installed his new wife. "It had most pleasant outlooks; in front over the garden of the Jesuits and beyond to Mount Royal; [on the east to the Château de

Drawn in the 1840s, this view shows Notre Dame Street with McGill's house the first building on the left. Nelson's column was erected just beyond, at the top of Jacques Cartier Square. Horse-drawn omnibuses, such as that shown outside the Château de Ramezay, were not introduced until after McGill's time, nor were the wooden sidewalks. Artist James Duncan.

Ramezay]; on the west over the garden of the Château de Vaudreuil; on the south, over the city wall, to the river and St Helen's Island."[21] James could not have given Charlotte a more desirable wedding present; at the same time, the purchase of that particular residence meant that in Montreal, James McGill had arrived – and meant to stay.

4 Montreal Merchant, 1778–1805

As McGill had hoped, the American War of Independence re-treated south from the St Lawrence valley, and the citizens of Montreal were left to get on with their own lives with remarkably little disturbance from the warring parties. Even the long supply line up the Ottawa River, down the waterways to Georgian Bay, and on to Mackinac (mercifully, the name had been shortened) resumed its normal activities, harassed only by its regular problems. Back in Montreal, James was able to plunge into the engrossing task of becoming a very active partner in the growing firm of Todd, McGill and Company.

The volume of fur exports from Quebec varied widely during the years 1770–90: the high point reached before the American invasion was followed by a considerable decline, then a sharp rebound after the retreat of 1776; as the War of Independence dragged on there was another fairly steady decline, though export levels remained above those of the pre-British period. The signing of the peace treaty in 1783 and the increasingly effective organization of the North West Company brought another sharp increase in the total volume of the fur trade to new record levels. While not sustained at this height, exports then remained well above the volumes of the years prior to 1776.[1] McGill's own participation in the fur trade during these years followed this general pattern; but the trade was becoming more complicated, with one trader buying skins from another, or acting as agent for another, and requiring separate accounts for them. Here is a letter from Todd, McGill to John Askin and Co., which records a series of financially satisfactory transactions but also reflects the uncertain conditions of the trade:

Montreal 11 October 1784.
Dear Sirs:

We now inclose you copies of the different Sales of Furrs shipped last year for your account, on which it is pleasing to remark there arises a very handsome profit viz

on those of mark B	....	£.794	1	7	stg
of purchase from Mcombs					
on do.	Mark A	....	34	6	2
on do.	JAA	....	41	19	5
on do.	JA-TWC	....	752	12	3
on do.	JBB Bathes	....	349	11	3
			1972	10	8

equal to £ 2 191 141 [Halifax] Currency carried to the Credit of your Account. It would afford us satisfaction could we hold out to you similar hopes against another year, but we fear much for deer Skins, as the quantity going home greatly exceeds that of last year & we are sorry to remark that those from the Messrs MaCombs turn out of very inferior quality, nor are the Raccons [sic] of this parcell any thing so good as those of last years and to add to these untoward circumstances there is yet near to 400 packs not come down, on which we fear an additional premium of 2 P[er]cen]t must be paid as there remains but small hopes of our being able to get them a board the vessels which are to sail from Quebec on the 25th Inst--

Ever since the arrival of our Mr Todd our time has been so much taken up with baling Furrs & promising Frends [i.e., providing funds] to answer the heavy drafts from above [i.e., up country], that we have not looked into the Accounts he brought down & we must now deferr it untill all the Shipping are gone.

We have now nearly made provision to get through the bussiness of this year with the same regard to your drafts as heretofore, that is, that no man can say he has ever called twice for money that was due--We think we may now flatter ourselves with things going on more smoothly in future & that we shall be more free from perplexity & anxiety than has been the case for two or three years past.

We have hitherto as you may have observed declined making any charge for our Trouble of shipping Furrs to England, tho' most certainly it creates more employment than importing Goods, nor is it our intention to make any charge on what is past, but on all future Shippments as well as those of this year we mean to make a charge of One & a Half per cent, which we daresay you will think reasonable for that kind of Agency-- The Merchants at home charge 2 ½ p/ct altho' they never see a Skin, whilst we are obliged to do every thing ourselves & we assure you it is not a small business to go properly through with--

> We are with much esteem
> Dear Sirs
> Your sincere Friends
> Todd & McGill[2]

There are some interesting points to be noted from this letter. Merchandise (and no doubt persons) on their way to London are said to be "going home," a tell-tale phrase; Todd and the furs seem to have arrived together, which suggests that Todd had been paying one of his visits to Mackinac – as well as making use of agents, the partners kept personally close to the trade. That was true in more ways than one. As McGill comments ruefully, "it was not a small thing to go through properly with." Handling the furs received from up country, sorting, assessing, and repacking them for their transatlantic voyage was a physically demanding job, heavy, smelly, and dirty. We can see James arriving early in the morning at his St Paul Street warehouse, doffing his jacket and donning a stout leather apron, and spending a long day sorting, hefting and stacking the heavy bales. If a ship was waiting, the day would be long indeed. A one and a half percent charge would not be unreasonable, epecially since the shippers would know that by using Todd, McGill's services, they could be assured that the job was "gone through properly with." Finally, there is the reference to accomodating friends "to answer the heavy drafts from above," to which we will return later.

Another example of trading relationships is an agreement dated 1778 whereby David McCrae and Co. of Mackinac named William and John Kay of Montreal their agents in that city, making them wholly responsible for receiving and selling McCrae's skins; but James McGill and his friend John Porteous were appointed evaluators of the skins. The Kays could sell them at the evaluators' price

A merchant travels with a canoe brigade to Michilimackinac.
Artist Illingworth Kerr.

or better and would receive a percentage commission. At some time in that same year,[3] the rivalry and at times bitter feuding between various competing traders and their partnerships had become so intense that some of the parties declared a truce and came together to pool their enterprises to form a cooperative, the famous North West Company. Probably at first the arrangements were fairly loose (Alexander Henry says they were contrived in the Northwest itself) but a year later the brothers Benjamin and Joseph Frobisher and Simon McTavish were the leading spirits in a more formal agreement reached in Montreal, in which Todd, McGill Company was also involved. Another participant was "McGill, Patterson," James' brother John and his partner. Seven partnerships, including the two McGill companies, took two shares each, and two others took one share each, making sixteen shares in all. Todd, McGill's relationship with the partnership can best be described as cautious. When the original sixteen shares were later expanded to forty-six, the Todd, McGill firm stayed with its original stake of two shares. James, we may be sure, approved of any agreement that removed impediments from the business of merchandising, and the cooperative agreement undoubtedly prevented unbridled competition from becoming open warfare, which it was threatening to do. It also strengthened the competitive position of the Montreal traders *vis-à-vis* the Hudson's Bay Company with whom in the far northwest the Montreal traders were finding themselves increasingly entangled. On the other hand, both Todd and McGill were at heart free enterprisers who valued their independence, so the part the Todd, McGill partnership played in the often turbulent story of the nor'westers was a minor one.

There were also other reasons for their slight involvement with the North West Company. The fur trade, as MacSporran remarks, had by the middle 1780s separated out into three main areas, Detroit (including the Ohio valley and Mississippi region), Mackinac (the Great Lakes region), and the Northwest, generally understood by this time as the country north and west of Lake Superior.[4] As the cooperative's name indicated, its main interest was in the third area. But from the late 1770s James McGill had interested himself more particularly in the Detroit and Mackinac areas. Although large quantities of pelts were still being brought in from more distant hunting grounds, the local fur trade in these areas

was declining, partly because of exhausted supplies but also because increased settlement was destroying the fur-bearing animals' habitat. But that same settlement furnished a growing
general trade on which McGill placed considerable reliance. The
fur trade, it was true, offered the richer rewards but he knew and
none better that it was always a precarious business. So many
things could go wrong.

The affairs of the North West Company were often in a state of
flux since the original agreements were for short periods only, at
the end of which new terms had to be renegotiated. But the association managed to continue and prosper, and Todd, McGill maintained an interest at least as sleeping partners until as late as 1803,
when they sold their two shares to McTavish, Frobisher and Co.
for eight thousand pounds.[5] By that time Todd had pretty well retired, while McGill had transferred the bulk of his business activities to his new firm, James and Andrew McGill, having taken his
younger brother as partner five years earlier. More will be said of
this second firm later, but in the middle 1780s when McGill was in
full stride as a merchant, his interests were already increasingly
centred upon Upper Canada and the Great Lakes.

As he settled into this new business, he must often have remarked, at least in his own mind, what a varied trade it was. Settlers needed household articles such as pots and pans, buckets,
domestic utensils, material for curtains, dresses, bedcovers, needles, cottons, scissors, as well as axes, ploughshares, spades, seed,
guns, powder, shot, fish hooks, lines, cords, ropes – the lists were
endless, the quantities small, the profit modest, the transport difficult to arrange, but the flow continuous, and McGill was not too
proud to handle a business of small but steady returns. One of his
most frequent customers was of course John Askin, up in Mackinac itself, and some of Askin's letters written in the summer of
1778 give us revealing glimpses of frontier life and of domestic
needs.[6] Here is an excerpt from a letter dated 8 May:

I do declare that as things go on now, I don't know what to order, of all I
write for nothing Arrives. I must leave all to Yourselves. If Liquors could
be got up, I mean Rum, by way of the lakes without being embezeled to
so great a degree, [I will take it] no matter how much you sent. However
I think there should be a man to take care of each Boat load or at most not
to have charge of more than two … Mrs Askin begs you'll be so kind as to

deliver Madame Perinault the piece of Silk with the trimmings, that are comeing or come from England for her, there's two pieces in the Memorandm, but one of them we suppose will be left Montreal before this reaches you. Madame Perinault will be so kind as to have the other made up for Mrs Askin.[7]

Evidently, John Askin wrote as he thought, and used capitals with a fine sense of freedom. It is also evident that frontier women, while as interested as women in general in matters of dress, had little opportunity to settle the details for themselves. On 28 May Askin wrote: "I owe Kitty her wedding Gown, as there was nothing here fit for it. Please have one made for her in the french fashion, of a light blue satin."[8] And 14 June: "Nous sommes fort sur Le Dernier Gout de Londres, you may judge of Mrs Askin and Mrs Robertson by other Ladies, for in certain matters women are almost all alike."

In matters of fashion that surely is a calumny that most women would deny and agree with in the same breath, since the whole object of the exercise is apparently to be alike and yet different at one and the same time. Did McGill attend to these matters of ladies' gowns personally, or did he enlist the aid of Mrs McGill with regard to these rather obscure directions? But sometimes Askin had requirements of his own. He wrote on 23 June: "I am in such want of Waistcoats and Breeches that I beg you will have immediately purchased for me six or eight Yards of fine white Cloth, which with suitable trimmings please send me by the very first oppertunity, hardly any person will refuse to embark so small a bundle on being paid for so doing, the kind of Buttons I would choose is plain gilt with Eyes if to be had, if not with Ivory bottoms, but eyes answers best as they can be taken off when washing. The Want of Breeches makes me dwell so long on the Subject in order to insure their comeing."

Askin was such a regular correspondent that no doubt McGill had learnt to read between the lines, and he evidently gave satisfaction for Askin was prepared "to leave all to Yourselves." Another June letter asks for two fiddles, "and please not to forget a quantity of strings." Evidently, culture was beginning to gain a toehold in frontier society.

The general trade must have taken a good deal of McGill's time and efforts, especially as Askin was by no means the only customer to be attended to. But the main business was still the gathering of furs from the scattered Indian trappers and bringing them down to Montreal for shipment to London. In that business great fortunes could be made – and as easily lost. This was particularly so in the unsettled years following the end of the American war. Many merchants failed in business at this time, and Todd, McGill themselves suffered from a cash-flow problem so severe that James feared the London suppliers would withhold further credit. He wrote in great urgency to Askin and no doubt to all their other creditors to pay quickly as much as they could muster. To Askin he wrote: "[I] conjure you by every tie of friendship to leave no stone unturned in order to make further remittances, for on this summer depends our existence as men of Character and Credit."[9] First Todd and then McGill took ship to Britain to deal with the crisis. He received generous accommodation from his suppliers, and years later in his will he left one thousand pounds to John Brickwood of London in recognition of a long and happy business association; no doubt he had this particular occasion very much in mind. Todd, McGill weathered the crisis but the experience increased James' reluctance to depend more on the fur trade than was necessary. In his opinion the opportunity to diversify lay in the growing settlement of Upper Canada and the Great Lakes basin.

One beneficial result of the late war for McGill was that he had developed a profitable business as a supplier to the British army. He was not called upon to furnish military stores, but he often provided bulk supplies of food and liquor to the army forts on the St Lawrence and the Great Lakes and met the needs of individual officers for such things as wine, spirits, tobacco, sugar, and, when they began to bring their ladies with them, cottons, needles, sheeting, and a hundred and one household necessities. The army posts at Oswegatchie, Kingston, Oswego, York, Detroit, and Mackinac needed local supplies of wheat, corn, rum, and the like, and in such matters Todd, McGill could prove themselves very useful. They were, of course, keen business men, sometimes perhaps too much so, for General Frederick Haldimand, while writing in 1779 to the commandant at Mackinac, Major Arent de Peyster, saw fit to warn him of the "rapacity" of Todd, McGill and Co.[10] Perhaps on occasion James and his partner had driven what the general considered too hard a bargain. But since they continued to get military business, their "rapacity" cannot have been too outrageous.

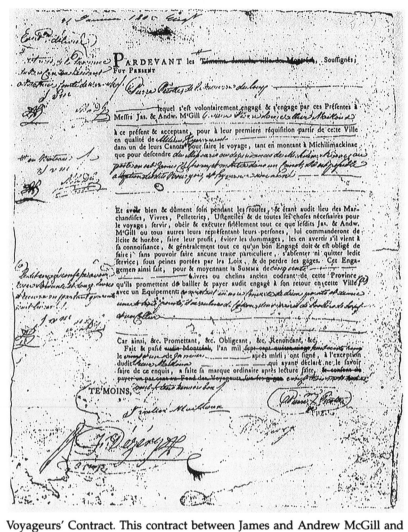

Voyageurs' Contract. This contract between James and Andrew McGill and Pierre Picotte is dated 21 January 1805. The notaries have used a printed form and amended it as required. It binds Picotte "to go by canoe or boat to the Missouri or the Michilimackinac area, and go up by canoe to the post where James Cleghorn is, and there winter for one year at a pay of 500 livres." Pierre could not sign but has made his mark. French is still the language of the fur trade and the pay remains modest.

Engaging men from Montreal and the surrounding parishes for service "up country" was another regular occupation. For one thing, there was the annual need to furnish voyageurs for the fur canoes. This continued well into the nineteenth century. In 1790, Todd, McGill engaged fifty-one men, not necessarily all for their own ventures, and in 1795 as many as eighty. The highest total was 127 in 1800, but thereafter numbers declined rapidly. Mac-Sporran comments as the years passed it became more difficult to recruit these men. McGill wrote in 1799 to Askin: "We hope you may derive benefit from these winteres, for the trouble of engaging them is beyond any compensation charged that belongs to merchants for such business."[11] But the firm often acted as employment agents for other companies and engagements for services other than those of the fur trade were not unusual. One versatile person named Louis Gareau was engaged in 1799 *en qualité de taillandier, Serurier et Maréchal ferrant*" (toolmaker, locksmith, and blacksmith) for the Compte de Puisaye, a French royalist who, to escape the dangers of the French Revolution, was establishing a royalist settlement in Windham, Upper Canada, about fifteen miles north-west of York.

Possibly this Gareau was not wholly satisfactory in his third occupation, or perhaps could not cope with all the work, for McGill that same year was still looking for a blacksmith for the count. He found a man called Jean Baptiste Vallières, equipped him and sent him off to Windham. Perhaps remembering his own family's involvement in the smithing craft, McGill took a particular interest in this commission, and indeed it was to prove a significant connection for his later affairs.[12]

Another such commission was the service McGill performed for Richard Cartwright, a pioneer in Kingston, who eventually became one of the foremost merchants in Upper Canada. He asked his friend in Montreal to receive in 1799 a young man from Scotland who was coming to Kingston to establish a school, primarily for the benefit of Cartwright's sons.[13] The schoolmaster's name was John Strachan. McGill's task was to look after him in Montreal, secure him conveyance upcountry, and outfit him for his journey and for his subsequent life in the frontier settlement. This McGill did with so much satisfaction on both sides that when later Strachan had taken orders in the Church of England and settled in a mission church in Cornwall, James on his journies upcountry often visited him in his rectory. Those visits to a young friend served more than one purpose and were to prove of considerable importance.[14] But McGill would never have known Strachan and formed this happy relationship had he not undertaken the commission to receive the dominie from Scotland and outfit him for his journey to Kingston.

The fact is that as a merchant, McGill was obviously ready to accept "any commission for a commission," and some of his undertakings seem very strange indeed. In 1787, for example, he was reimbursed by the Department of Indian Affairs for various expenditures he had made in the government's interests, including a payment to a Jacques Lefrenier for the cost of four slaves, presumably Indians, whom Lefrenier had purchased to hand over to other Indians as replacements for those lost by the tribe in a battle, while fighting on the British side in the late war. It is specifically mentioned that this transaction was undertaken to fulfil a promise made by the local British commander.[15] This item in McGill's accounts reminds us that slavery, although not a prominent institution in Canada, nevertheless was not formally illegal in the province, and existed widely among the Indians. In the southern United States and in the West Indies, of course, enslavement of Africans and the use of indentured labour of men and women shipped from England were both recognized formally. In fact, the gradation of ranks between servants, indentured servants, and outright slaves was often in practice much blurred. John Askin drew up an agreement between himself and a woman who entered his service, that she would faithfully serve him as master and do all that was bidden of her for a year, and in return he would feed and shelter her and give her a black dress. No reference to wages is included, which makes the engagement sound very much like term indenture. But when the alternative for a lone woman was death by starvation in Canada's cold winter, the choice was clear.[16]

Even in Montreal, living conditions were often primitive, and to be a member of a household and so be at least ensured of shelter and food was better than outright destitution. Moreover, James McGill was not ahead of his times in social matters. He was acquainted with Thomas Paine's *Rights of Man* and considered it (in the context, it must be remembered, first of the American War of Independence and then of the French Revolution) to have "turned peoples heads."[17] One reason stressed in the petitions he signed for English schools in Montreal was that at present boys were often sent south to American schools, where they might be indoctrinated with ideas of republicanism and democracy. With regard to the institution of slavery, McGill must have been very familiar with it during his Indian trading years, and if he spent some years in the Carolinas, he lived in a society where slavery was very much part of the social fabric. So when we hear that in 1788 he purchased from Jean Cavilhe at a cost of fifty-six pounds a negress named Sarah, aged about twenty-five, to be a servant in his household, it must be remembered that McGill was conforming to the mores of his time. He was generously ready to administer the city's care of foundlings and those adjudged insane, and he would, as we shall see, personally care for the widow and the orphan, but he was not a social reformer. No doubt Sarah was well treated in the McGill household, but the fact remains that she was purchased and owned as a slave.[18] James McGill was a man of the eighteenth century, not of the twentieth.

One constant problem for the military in Canada was a shortage of cash. The officers received drafts payable in English pounds by the paymaster general in Quebec, but they needed cash to pay merchants like John Askin in Mackinac or Todd, McGill in Montreal. The remarks in the 1784 letter to John Askin about "the heavy drafts from above" and "the bussiness this year with regard to your drafts" refer to the same difficulty. Canada at this time had no banks, and at least three of the many petitions McGill signed urged the establishment of a banking system. But the government did not welcome the idea, thinking perhaps that it would increase the economic influence of the participating merchants too greatly. Also, the French Canadian seigneurs and their clergy (the latter had inherited the medieval distrust of "usury") feared that a banking system would encourage British domination of the provincial economy and therefore favoured the government's inactivity in the matter.[19] As a result, despite his many efforts, the Bank of Montreal was not founded until four years after McGill's death. So all his lifetime, McGill kept considerable amounts of cash in his strongroom and transferred government paper into smaller, more convenient bills of exchange, or into cash, but of course charging a commission for doing so. On occasion prominent persons such as Chief Joseph Brant and Sir John

Johnson, the general superintendent of Indian Affairs, were glad to avail themselves of McGill's financial services, but more frequently his clients were serving men of lesser rank, including the junior officers. In this regard at least, the Montreal merchants were already fulfilling some banking functions, and McGill was one of those resorted to most often.

All this is amply illustrated by the James and Andrew McGill Company commercial journal for the period 1798–1800. The journal provides a direct view into the transactions and business dealings of the firm that James initiated as the successor, in some respects, to Todd, McGill and Company, though the original firm continued in existence, largely to provide for ongoing arrangements that it was not convenient to terminate. The journal, it will be observed, comes from the later years of McGill's merchant career: earlier commercial records have not survived.[20] This is not so disturbing as might otherwise have been the case, because it is evident from the journal that the successor firm picked up from where its predecessor was leaving off, and that the kinds of transactions were as varied as ever. The journal logged every transaction for the day, whatever its nature, but in the margin is noted the number of the particular account to which the item must be transferred. So since one numbered account was evidently "Jas McGill Domestic" and another "Andrew McGill Domestic," one can observe many homely items mixed in with major business deals. W.D. Lighthall, who first brought the book to scholarly attention, attempted a short description of its heterogeneous contents and what can be learned from them. He points to the evidence that the McGills had as their agent in Kingston, Richard Cartwright, John Askin in Detroit, Phyn Ellice and Company in London; that they had their own branch house in Mackinac; their correspondents in Quebec, Niagara, New York, and the West Indies; and colleagues and friends throughout the West as far as Great Slave Lake and the Pacific. Their own large revenues are recorded in the journal, as well as many personal details of their manner of living, the names of their house servants, masons, ironworkers, tailors, painters, and other tradesmen. According to Lighthall, one can even compile from this document the roll of physicians in Montreal at the turn of the century and gain a fair idea of current medical practices and remedies. In its pages one comes across the names of the numerous ships that carried the McGill furs through the

Upper Lakes or from Quebec across the Atlantic, or transported grain, hides, fish, rum, sugar, and tobacco to and from the West Indies; the whole detail of the voyageur operation is laid out, including the purchase of wampum in New York for the trade with the Indian tribes. We are familiarized with articles of dress for both men and women, the furniture imported from England, and the repairs and additions to Burnside Place. Other items of interest are McGill's subscriptions to the Beaver Club; his generous gifts to widows, orphans, employees, and victims of fires; his presents to his sister Margaret in Glasgow, to the sons and daughters of his friends – "Board and education of little A. Todd" – and to his own wife and stepchildren: all these afford a very good picture of James McGill in his office and in his home.[21]

A further picture of McGill in both countinghouse and home, together with a rare glimpse of his easy, intimate relations with Isaac Todd, is provided by a letter he wrote to his friend in 1805 while Todd was away from home, probably in New York. The letter also gives examples of the merchants' banking functions, and reveals that, even at that late date, maintaining credit in London and securing adequate returns from debtors "up country" was still a matter of considerable anxiety:

Montreal, 17 October, 1805

My dear Todd,

It is time I should begin to give you some account of the matters you left with me or my House [i.e., J & A McGill Co.]. Seeing that Campbells' Furs would not in my estimation be worth 46.000 Livres and Forsyth and Co. being holders for 26.000 and Pothier for 22.000, I prevailed with [John] Richardson to become the Shipper [and] to settle with Pothier; but they go under our Insurance to Messrs. Inglis Ellice and Co. Mr [John Jacob] Astor has been here [and] purchased largely (I believe for £11,000) of Otter, Beaver and Martins and settled with Messrs Parker, Gerrard, Ogilvy and Co., also Messrs Henderson and Armour. He acquainted me with this, informing me at the same time that he had never charged the Teas to you but to them, and therefore has no claim on you, which is noted in your Balance Sheet. As to the Balance of £226 you were owing him, he has added Interest and drawn on us for it, which we of course shall pay ...

The little Girls Jane and Agnes are very well and whenever [I may be] called upon for any thing they may want as well as their boarding they shall not be neglected. The little Boy who is now visibly mending, has occupied us all so much at times [as] to give much pain and chagrin ...

I have now to speak of our own matters but not yet having accounts I cannot do it with precision as usual. I think however as before mentioned that our Debt at home will amount to £41.000 Sterling of which we [shall] remitt by estimation £25,000; this is not as usual and you will readily believe gives no pleasure. Remittances from the Indian Trade have been very bad. Messrs McGregor who sent us last year £11,000 do not [this year] exceed £4,500 currency; their account will be rather against them, than in their favor at the end of the year. Giasson [?] and Berthlot from whom I expected from £12 to £14 Thousand currency will hardly reach to Ten, and as to Mr Dickson you know already in part how [his account] stands, but more on this subject in another letter. No money [profit?] has been got for Rum as usual, indeed we have luckily imported but 3 tuns; it has been sold at 5 shillings [per gallon?] or even 4 shillings and 6 pence in large parcels, tho the worth is 5 shillings and 10 pence. With dry Goods [i.e., clothing] we are stocked too much and shall import few indeed another year, but the remedy does not prevent Interest from accumulating. In short unless the value of Furs goes up there is no saying where it will end – we must hope for better times and as the [wheat] Crop of Upper Canada is said to be good, it is more likely that payments will prove pretty full next year, more especially as it has been written from England that wheat [there] has risen to a high price. I flatter myself with hearing from you by the September packet and before Navigation shuts and I hope to learn that you had got well. You are much missed here, and your return will be anxiously looked for, but by none more than, My Dear Todd,

Your sincere Friend
James McGill[22]

It is clear from this letter that although by 1805 McGill was beginning to lessen his involvement in the fur trade, it was still a matter of considerable interest and concern to him. Nevertheless we know from other evidence that at the turn of the century the changes in McGill's merchant activities were becoming more marked.

Land deals in particular were beginning to assume more importance. John Cooper the regards Detroit land purchases, effected between 1797 and 1805, as signalling McGill's entry into systematic land speculation. Earlier acquisitions had been made haphazardly: a farm at L'Assomption, Lower Canada, a water lot at William Henry (Sorel), Montreal properties including a distillery, and of course Burnside, his summer home at the foot of Mount Royal. From 1801, however, land was secured methodically; that year McGill acquired 10,000 acres in Hunterstown Township and 32,400 acres in Stanbridge Township, and it was probably in this period that land was secured in Upper Canada near Kingston and York.[23]

"McGill's business career," points out John Cooper, "epitomized much of the economic development of Lower Canada in the late eighteenth century." In the 1770s, 1780s, and 1790s the warehouses on Rue St Paul were the centre of the McGill fur-trading empire; in 1803, however, as Cooper remarks, it was Lord Selkirk's impression that McGill had retired from the fur trade, although remaining in what Selkirk called "the ordinary Colonial trade." His lordship was somewhat too previous, but nevertheless a shrewd observer. Other interests – imports and exports, land dealings, the embryo functions of banking – were indeed progressively replacing the older commerce. In 1796 Todd, McGill and Company were exporting squared timber to London,[24] and it is not surprising that McGill was one of the merchants who advocated the purchase and operation of ships especially for the Montreal-Atlantic crossing. "By such means," concludes Cooper, "in a changing economic environment did James McGill and his fellow merchants assure the metropolitan supremacy of Montreal."[25] James McGill was not only a citizen of Montreal: he had become one of those who shaped its destiny.

5 The New Neighbour, 1778–93

We have been looking at McGill as a merchant and his evolving interests right through to the later stages of his career. But it is necessary to return to his earlier days to understand his attitude towards the American Revolution and his concerns as a man of business with the immense question of Canada's boundaries. The previous chapter began by recording that in 1776 the American War of Independence receded from the St Lawrence valley, leaving the citizens of Montreal to get on with their lives in peace. But of course they constantly received news of the varying fortunes in the struggle, and their emotions were affected very differently according to the degree that their sympathies or personal interests, or in not a few cases members of their families, were involved. The French-speaking population as a whole probably felt no great concern, but their clergy at least viewed every republican success with renewed alarm: they already sensed vibrations of the coming upheaval in France; the British patriots and sympathisers with the American Tory loyalists experienced a see-saw of emotions as the fortunes of war ebbed and flowed; as a merchant, McGill knew full well that his personal enterprises were very much at hazard in its outcome, and he followed events closely.

His sympathies were of course strongly with the loyalists. Throughout the conflict, the British held, more or less unchallenged, the forts of Oswegatchie, Oswego, Detroit, and Mackinac, as well as (after the debacle of 1775–76) those of the more clearly

Canadian territories. As a valuable part of his trade was in supplying the needs of the military personnel of the outposts, McGill also
had good commercial reasons for supporting the British government and its representatives. However, the Indian trade and its
valuable commerce in furs was still the most lucrative part of his
enterprise, and as long as he could send canoes up to Detroit and
Mackinac, he continued annually to lay out considerable sums for
the trade, both in the Ohio valley and for the "North West," which
in 1770s usage included a vast area south of Lake Superior.[1] As
long as the British occupation of Detroit and Mackinac was not
threatened – and there was little American activity in "the West"
and "North West," as the thirteen colonies then interpreted those
terms – McGill's commerce was relatively undisturbed, and
through the war years he traded steadily up country and on balance did well. As we have seen, it was a serious cash-flow problem
in the immediate postwar years that strained his resources. Naturally, he resented the war because it was a further complication to
be taken into account in his trading activities.

But in his assessment of the American Revolution there was another consideration which also weighed greatly with him. He saw
the formerly prosperous, developing communities of the thirteen
colonies plunged into uncertainty and confusion by the war, the
worst aspect of which was its divisive effect on close neighbours.
The American War of Independence was a civil conflict as well as
an anti-imperial war. Respectable, established citizens, substantial
merchants, solid proprietors, and landowners were deprived of
their property, often by their own neighbours; their wives and
children were banished from their homes, in many cases even subjected to mob violence; on the other side, American families were
ruthlessly attacked by brutal mercenaries in British pay or mur-
dered by their Indian allies. And for what? McGill would ask.
Some abstract notion of independence! As the Congress struggled
to establish a monetary system and found itself being plunged
deeper and deeper into debt, losing all financial credibility in a sea
of worthless paper, McGill contrasted the unhappy American
scene with the peace and prosperity of Canada and the solid
strength of the British pound. He failed utterly to understand the
depth of conviction in the Adamses, Jeffersons, and Washingtons
of the revolutionary leadership. These men were prepared to
pledge, as the Declaration of Independence avowed, their "Lives,

Fortunes and Sacred Honor" to the republican ideal. "Unlike most revolutions that followed, this one was distinguished by a deep concern for, and emphatic stress upon, legality. The Americans fought for the rights they believed were guaranteed them as Englishmen under the British constitution, and for the rights of man as they understood them to be derived from the 'Laws of Nature and of Nature's God.'"[2] That was something that James McGill did not, could not, understand. Under the British Crown he enjoyed a settled order of society, liberty to worship as he pleased, and freedom to conduct his affairs without undue interference, the right to protest unfair laws, and the protection of the courts against bureaucratic tyranny – a protection to which he himself had appealed on at least one occasion – and in general a system of law and order that, since no constitution is perfect, he had strenuously sought to improve. What more could this republican revolution at so fearful cost hope to achieve than a constitutional monarchy had already given?

This antipathy to the American Revolution grew even stronger as he saw the favourable outcome of the miltary conflict incline more and more towards the America contenders. The British effort lacked the support of public opinion at home, was ineptly conducted by incompetent commanders, and, after 1778, did not engage the full attention of a government distracted by war with France, Spain, and the Netherlands. After the disastrous surrender of Cornwallis and his forces at Yorktown in 1781 there was little doubt as to the final outcome of the conflict.

What was left very much in doubt, however, was the boundary that would be determined between the Province of Quebec and this new nation, the United States of America, and equally in question were the trading agreements that would be sanctioned between them. If, as was rumoured, the line were to be drawn in such a way that the military posts at Oswego, Detroit, and Mackinac were to be surrendered to the Americans, and if Canadians were to be barred from trading with Indians through those settlements, Montreal's merchants would suffer an immense reverse. In 1783 a committee of London merchants engaged in the Canadian trade exerted itself energetically to influence the outcome of the negotiations, with the object of having the boundary drawn further south. Isaac Todd, speaking of course also for his partner James McGill, was in London with other Montreal merchants to support their efforts. But the British government, hoping to gain favour with the Americans and woo them from their alliance with France, disregarded the Canadian pleas.

The negotiations took place in Paris, far away from the vast areas under discussion. On the one side were British negotiators who had slight personal knowledge of the issues at stake and on the other Americans led by Benjamin Franklin, who had nursed a plan to annex all of Canada to the United States ever since his sojourn in Montreal in 1775. The negotiations were hampered by deficient maps, but the Americans' greater familiarity with the country, and their much closer personal interest, gave them immense advantages. However, the British were not ready to quit North America entirely, so Franklin and his friends failed in their attempt to secure the whole of Canada. They then proposed two alternative boundaries from which, they said, Great Britain could choose. Both proposals began with the St Croix River on the Nova Scotia coast and then followed the height of land between the St Lawrence and its tributaries, and the rivers running into the Atlantic Ocean, until the line of demarcation reached the forty-fifth parallel, where it turned to run along that line until it met the St Lawrence. Here the two proposals diverged radically. According to the first alternative the boundary was to continue to be the forty-fifth parallel stretching as far as the Mississippi River, beyond which lay the dominions of Spain; according to the second, the boundary was to follow the line of the Great Lakes and their connecting rivers to the Lake of the Woods. Only from that point would it run due west to the Mississippi. "In the end," commented Donald Creighton, "the British chose the second alternative, not apparently because of any interest in the enormous issues involved, but simply because the water boundary looked more definite."[3]

The first of these two lines would have left Quebec deprived of the Niagara Peninsula and with only difficult and relatively unprofitable access to the Great Lakes; it is doubtful whether the truncated colony would have been economically viable. The British government certainly had to reject that proposition. But even the second line can only be described as an unconscionable land grab. It fell far short of what the Quebec and Montreal merchants thought proper: that the St Lawrence River and Great Lakes should remain what they had been historically, a truly Canadian asset. It has to be remembered that most of the area under discussion was still virgin forest and unsettled and, apart from the aboriginal inhabitants, had been almost exclusively explored and harvested by men of Montreal, first French and latterly Canadien and British. McGill and his friends thought therefore that both the lines proposed by the Americans should have been rejected. They favoured a line following the watershed of the Great Lakes to the south of Lake Erie. From that point, they really wanted the old 1774 Quebec Act boundary, which would have given Canada the whole of the Ohio valley, but they were prepared *faute de mieux* to settle for a line which proceeded west until it reached a tributary of the Mississippi and then followed the west bank of the great river up to the borders of Prince Rupert's Land and the domains of the Hudson's Bay Company.

This was by no means an unreasonable proposition. The British still held the forts of Oswegatchie, Oswego, Niagara, Miami, Detroit, Mackinac, and the post at Grand Portage. At that point in time, therefore, physical possession as well as history, to say nothing of Indian treaty obligations, were certainly on the Canadian side of the argument. Yet the British accepted the second American proposal; as Creighton says: "With a few casual strokes of the pen, Great Britain ceded an empire which the colony of the St Lawrence had built by over a century of effort."[4] The fur traders, who had restored and managed at great cost and effort the one business which had sustained Canada from the beginning, were carelessly disregarded while the western Indians, who had been solemnly guaranteed the possession of their lands, were callously betrayed. Similarly, G.F. Stanley points out how delicately the fate of Canada had trembled in the balance: "For one brief moment the British representative almost succumbed to Franklin's winning ways, but when the treaty was signed the terms did not put Canada within the boundaries of the United States."[5] But, he adds, the Americans did get away with a huge area of Canadian territory. "The Ohio valley, a region historically part of Canada and linked geographically and economically with the St Lawrence River system and Montreal, was wrenched from Canada and incorporated into the United States."[6]

Like Creighton, Stanley emphasizes that this was done even though the British were still in full military possession of the area. The prevailing view in London seems to have been that it did not

Quebec, 1774 Boundary and Northern Boundary Proposed by the United States

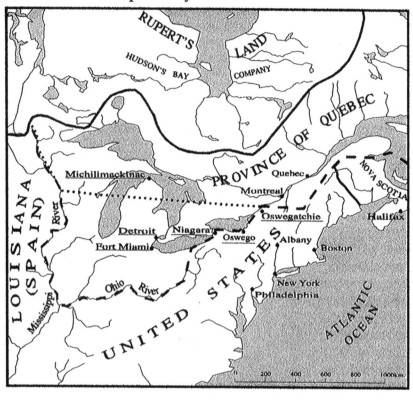

— — — 1774 to 1783
(Quebec Act
and Carleton's
Instructions)

——————— Other Boundaries

· · · · · · · · Northern Boundary
Proposal Offered by
the United States

Principal post retained by Britain
until evacuated in 1796: Oswego

Quebec, Boundary Wanted by Merchants and as Agreed to in 1783

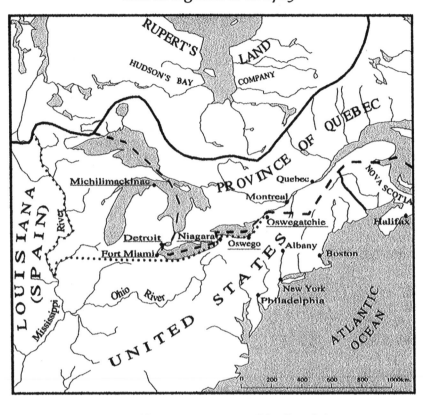

· · · · · · · · As Wanted by   ───────── Other Boundaries
               Merchants

─ ─ ─ ─ As Settled   Principal post retained by Britain
         in 1783   until evacuated in 1796: Oswego

matter greatly who had political control of the lands, since in either case England as the industrial power would be supplying and benefiting from the commerce, a view that proved to be short-sighted and mistaken. The British belatedly recognized that had they held on to the Ohio valley, the native tribes there could have constituted a buffer between the intrusive United States and the fledgling settlements in Upper Canada. Consequently, they retained the forts in the disputed lands until 1796, giving the native leaders grounds to hope that the treaty decision of 1783 might yet be reversed. This delay also gave merchants like Todd, McGill and Company reason even as late as 1791 and 1792 to address memoranda to Governor G.J. Simcoe of Upper Canada, urging the need for treaty revision and the retention of the Ohio valley or at least of the Great Lakes basin.[7] One must reflect that had the merchants had their way, the resultant two parts of British North America would doubtless have developed as far more equal partners, to the ultimate benefit of both. American imperialistic policies were a matter of great concern to James McGill in 1783 and would return thirty years later to challenge him even more severely.

The actual frontier line west of Detroit was left unsettled in some details in 1783 because it was recognized that the available maps were undependable. Of equal importance, the matter of reciprocal trading rights in the disputed territories was also left as a matter for further discussion. This at least left the Canadians free to continue trading at the traditional posts but only under the threat that the trading rights might be denied them when the matter was finally settled.[8] McGill had once declared that if Detroit were surrendered to the Americans he would at once cease trading there, but he later came to the view that so long as the reciprocal rights were allowed, the Montreal merchants, because of their superior connections, resources, and expertise, could still operate there with considerable profit and indeed continue to dominate the trade on both the Canadian and American sides of the line. This comes out clearly in a letter he wrote in August 1785 (that is, after the first partial determination of the new frontier) to the then lieutenant governor of the province, Henry Hamilton. McGill's immediate purpose in this letter was to persuade Hamilton to lift continuing wartime restrictions on Great Lakes trading, and especially the prohibition on the use of sailing vessels by private traders. These ships had begun to appear on the lakes in the early

1770s, but traders had been forbidden to use them during the war lest the boats should fall into American hands and be deployed against the British. However, McGill's longer-term concern was with the matter of reciprocal trading rights, and while his first interest there was the fur trade, one can be sure that in his own mind he was also thinking of general trade. The letter reveals incidentally that the "Indian trade" had not, apart from the introduction of these vessels, greatly changed in method or character from when he himself had first ventured into it. The following copy has been shortened and edited in one or two places to clear up minor obscurities.

1 August 1785.

In my last [letter] I partly anticipated yours of the 29th, relative to the probability of the trade to the post of Detroit & its dependencies falling soon into the hands of the Americans if private vessels were permitted [to Canadian traders] on the lakes ... You will be good enough to remark that the Upper Country trade in General, as now carried on from this place [Montreal] is extended as far South as the mouth of the Ohio, to the Westward as far as the Rivers falling from that side of the Mississippi will carry Canoes ... in Latitude 33°S to the sources of the Mississippi, and to the North-west as far as Lake Athabaska including the whole North side of Lake Huron & Superior [i.e., Montreal was currently exploiting the huge area of the Upper Mississippi well into the Spanish territory of Louisiana, the Ohio valley and the whole Great Lakes basin]. The Value of the whole [trade] I esteem at £180,000 Currency[9] ... & I believe that I am no £20,000 on either side of the reality – £100,000 value I think is brought from the Country now within the American Line as fix'd by the late treaty of Peace; the other £80,000 I consider as being within our own Line. If this statement is nearly just & I am satisfied to risk my reputation upon it as a merchant, the question will be, whether the Americans are likely to take away any part of our trade when they shall have got possession of the posts & have Vessels on the lakes or whether we are not more likely by having posts on the same Lakes & Vessels to interfere with them.

For my own part I am clearly of opinion that it must be a very long time before they can even venture on the smallest part of our trade, for the little [commerce in furs] that is to be had in the tract of Country lying between Lakes Ontario, Erie and Huron as South Boundaries, & the Ottawa River, Lake Nipissing & its discharge into Lake Huron as Northern Boundaries, can only be obtained by traders going up the different Rivers which water that tract of Country, there passing the Winter & trading with the Indians. And this can only be done in Birch Canoes, which will require [the Americans] a long time to become accustomed to, exclusive of the Legal impediment of trading in a country to which they are Aliens. The same reasons are applicable to the trade on the North shores of Huron & Superior & the North-West trade ... These Circumstances being considered, what are the reasons that could induce the traders [working] this Country to dispose [to Americans] of their fine furrs which are got within our lines? Will the Americans pay a higher price for them than can be obtained in London? No! And were they desirous of tempting with a higher offer, No man in his senses would [give them credit], and surely they cannot carry up money to [pay cash]. Besides it is well known that were these fine furrs to fall into their hand in any quantity, they must send them to England for a market as amongst themselves the consumption is very trifling. We may therefore infer that there is little probability of the Americans rivaling us soon in the tract which legally belongs to the Province, were they even allowed a free Competition.

It remains to consider how far we may interfere with the trade within their line and by what means, should the Americans under pain of confiscation prohibit all British Subjects from trading in the Indian Country within their Line. I make no doubt that the greatest part of the traders who are now at Detroit will become American Subjects, because they will thereby keep in their hands the trade they at present pursue ... But at the same time, if we can afford [to sell] Goods at Detroit cheaper than they can & are enabled to give better prices for furrs and Peltries, the traders on their side will fall on means to do bussines with us even at Detroit, notwithstanding any regulations they may make to the contrary ...

In short I am decidedly of Opinion that no part whatever of the Trade belonging to this Province by the treaty of Peace is likely to fall into the hands of the Americans but on the contrary that we may get a considerable part of theirs.[10]

This letter provides a good illustration of McGill's merchant mind at work, and reveals much of his character: his pride in his status as a merchant, his thorough grasp of the details of the complicated, far-ranging commerce in which he was engaged, and, in common with his colleagues of the North West Company, the courage with which he was prepared to engage in it.

The questions of the further western boundaries and of reciprocal trading rights were not settled until Jay's Treaty was signed in

1794, which confirmed that the former main fur-trading centres, Detroit, Mackinac, and Grand Portage, were in American territory. But the British did not in fact withdraw from the posts until 1796 and even then, by the terms of the treaty, Canadians were allowed reciprocal trading rights in the ceded territories. So James McGill and his fellow merchants were able to continue to dominate the Great Lakes commerce well into the nineteenth century, by which time the interests of the fur trade had definitely turned to the far Northwest. Its future was to lie with the North West Company, and the cooperative's great competitor was to be not the Americans but rather "the foe from the north," the Hudson's Bay Company. That rivalry was to continue long past James McGill's lifetime. However, his shrewd confidence in his own city's superiority in the fur trade and in Great Lakes trading in general was amply confirmed when the Hudson's Bay Company, having in 1821 absorbed the last of the old nor'westers, then found it expedient to move its own North American headquarters to Montreal, whence the company ruled its vast domains and, for another century, powerfully influenced the destiny of Canada from sea to sea.[11]

6 Magistrate and Citizen, 1778–1811

In the Glasgow in which James McGill had grown up, there were two classes of citizens to whom more ordinary mortals were expected to defer – the rich merchants of whom we have already heard, and the city magistrates. In the late medieval period, the "bailies," as these magistrates were called, demanded great respect: a man who failed to make way for them, or doff his hat, could well find himself in jail. James grew up familiar with the legend that a Robert McGill, no doubt a distant kinsman, once had the temerity, probably being drunk at the time, to threaten a bailie with a dagger. He was thrown in irons into the "tolbooth" (city jail) and kept there for the duration of the magistrate's pleasure; thereafter he had to appear barefoot and bareheaded at the Market Cross and on his knees beg forgiveness, pay a fine of one hundred Scots pounds, and suffer banishment from the city for seven years.[1] While by the mid-eighteenth century some of the formalities may have eroded, the society in which James grew up was still one where magistrates and civil rulers were highly respected and endowed with far-reaching powers. It was natural, therefore, that when he became a member of the Commission for the Peace in Montreal, he should take the responsibilities and dignity of his office seriously and expect others to do the same.

The role of magistrate was many sided. In the absence of a town council (Montreal was not incorporated and given a mayor and aldermen until 1832) the magistrates ordered the life of the city in accordance with custom and the regulations they as a body saw fit to introduce. The place and the days of markets within the city, the licensing of taverns and of ferries across the St Lawrence, the price of staples such as bread, the provision and upkeep of public wells and pumps, the organization and control of a constabulary, the provision and maintenance of a jail, the care of foundlings and the insane, the upkeep of roadways and the city walls – all came within the purview of the Commission of the Peace. In time of serious disturbance a magistrate could read the Riot Act and then call upon the military authorities to enforce the peace.[2] In court the magistrates, sitting weekly two at a time, heard any matters civil or criminal involving matters valued up to ten pounds – a considerable sum; they could deal with a case summarily, or remit it to the Quarter Sessions, presided over by two local justices of the peace, or send it to the next higher court, the Court of Common Pleas. Cases concerned with matters beyond the value of ten pounds were presented directly to this court, which was specifically designed by Governor Murray in 1764 to serve French Canadian needs. Canadien lawyers could practise in it, and on the bench were local amateur judges who spoke French and who were chosen because they shared Murray's benevolent attitude to the Canadiens.[3] Finally, a case could be appealed before the royal judges of the Court of King's Bench. Some of the magistrates' enactments required the endorsement of the Legislative Council[4] in Quebec City and, as noted, their court judgments could always be appealed to higher authorities; but even so in the daily life of the city the magistrates were a very influential body.

James McGill was appointed a member of the Commission of the Peace in 1776. He was a conscientious and hardworking member for twenty years until, in 1796, he was appointed to the higher rank of justice of the peace, in which capacity he sat at the Quarter Sessions to hear cases of a more serious nature.

There was yet another body established in Montreal – the grand jury. This body, empanelled *ad hoc* for specific charges, heard only the case for the prosecution to decide whether the charges were sufficiently well founded for a full trial to be ordered; but it had great latitude as to other recommendations it could make. In 1778, James McGill was appointed foreman of one such jury. In a province still struggling to legitimize its legal institutions and provide for an equitable dispension of justice, the case in question had considerable significance. The background is as follows. When the 1774 Quebec Act added the huge area of the Ohio-Mississippi triangle to the province's jurisdiction, three civil governorships were established in the new territories at Detroit, Vincennes, and Kaskaskia, but with little determination of the governor's responsibilities or powers. The outbreak of the American war further increased the difficulties of communication with Quebec, and like his colleagues at Vincennes and Kaskaskia, Henry Hamilton at Detroit had to rely upon his own judgment in many administrative matters.

One of his decisions was to continue to recognize Phillipe Dejean, a local magistrate whose tenure of office was much in question. Dejean, it was alleged, had carried out his duties in a tyrannical and arbitrary manner, particularly in passing the death sentence in 1776 on a man and a woman for the crime of robbery. The charge against Dejean was brought before McGill's grand jury, which not only brought in a verdict of "true bill" – that is, that the charges against Dejean were well founded and that he should be brought to trial – but went further and indicted Governor Henry Hamilton as the superior officer who had upheld the magistrate and confirmed the sentences. Whatever the rights and wrongs of the case might have been, the verdict was a courageous instance of concerned citizens, led by a man who firmly believed in the principle of justice for all, protesting vigorously against any abuse of power by bureaucrats, even though the alleged actions had taken place two years earlier, hundreds of miles distant in a frontier settlement very difficult of access, and in a time of war. The higher legal authorities in Montreal gave more weight to these considerations and decided not to prefer the charges, especially as in the interval Hamilton and Dejean had both been captured by American forces and were by then prisoners of war.[5]

The incident illustrates McGill's forthrightness. But it also placed him in a very embarrassing situation when Hamilton reappeared in Canada only six years later as lieutenant governor and administrator of the Province. It will be recalled that the following year, 1785, McGill wrote to Hamilton concerning trade restrictions and the current boundary discussions. This letter, cited in the previous chapter, was clearly part of an ongoing correspondence in which the two men were collaborating harmoniously, and McGill signed himself "your affectionate and very humble servant"; the

This early view shows the harbour as James McGill knew it, including the first steamboats introduced by John Molson 1809. There were no wharves until Molson built the first in 1816. Construction of permanent docks began in 1830. Artist R.A. Sproule.

"very humble" is simply an eighteenth-century convention, but the "affectionate" suggests a degree of warmth and regard in their relationship. Evidently, Hamilton bore no grudge against McGill for the grand-jury indictment, which speaks well of the governor's character and was extremely fortunate for James. It is not surprising that he came to have a warm regard for the man.

The grand jury of 1778 was but one of the assignments and responsibilities that the merchant magistrate was starting to accumulate. He was becoming recognized as the kind of person who could and would take on the tasks and commissions which in any city are necessary for the communal well-being. In 1780, for example, he sat on a tribunal that was considering the case of one Joseph Howard who was charged with unlicensed trading at Mackinac; the sentence was a fine of fifty louis, which suggests that due forms were observed and a wrist slapped. Three years later, when his commission as magistrate was renewed, he also accepted appointment as one of the commissioners for the city jail. This was certainly no sinecure, as we shall hear later.

While engaged in these important civic matters, McGill also had time to join with his neighbours in more practical schemes to improve matters in their own affairs. One of the constant hazards in Montreal was fire; the magistrates had already recommended that no more wooden houses and sheds should be built in the city. Although stone was being used increasingly for new building, the cold winters and the use of open wood fires to heat homes combined to keep the occurrence of house burnings all too frequent. Warehouses in which merchants' goods were stored were often at the same risk. In response, some concerned citizens, including James McGill, organized in 1786 the Montreal Fire Club. Its articles of association read in part as follows:

Considering the great Loss and Damage which happens to the property of Individuals in case of Fire for want of regulations for packing and moving Goods in Houses and Stores in danger,

We the Subscribers agree to form ourselves into a Fire Club for the mutual relief and assistance of each other under the following regulations, viz

1. The Club shall not consist of more than Fourteen members ...

2. Each member shall be provided with four good Leather Buckets and Four Bags of a Yard wide and a Yard and a half long marked FIRE CLUB No. I with his name at length, to be kept at their dwelling Houses and not to be used either of them on any other occasion than Fires ...

7. Each member shall acquaint himself with the Houses and stores of all the members of the Club and the different ways of access to them and in case of Fire they shall repair as soon as may be possible, to the place most in danger with their Bags and Buckets and shall there distribute themselves in different parts of the Buildings.[6]

James McGill took an active interest in this club; he was appointed its deputy steward in 1791 and steward the following year. The steward's duties were to see that members obeyed the rules and attended the quarterly meetings with their equipment ready for inspection. Delinquents were to be fined one shilling. However, a note was added at the end of the articles: "It is to be remembered that Mr James McGill and Mr Benjamin Frobisher's Office of Magistrate not allowing of particular attention from them to the Members of the Club in case of fire, their partners are added to supply their places." This suggests that McGill had someone deputize for him at the actual fires. No doubt each member hurried to the site with his buckets and bags and two or three hefty young men prepared to douse flames and remove goods (hence the bags) as directed by the member. The intention was not only to extinguish the blaze, if possible, but equally to prevent spoilage and looting, so it was important that the member or his officially recognized deputy be there himself. To further tighten security, anyone active at the fire site could be challenged for the club password, which was changed each year. In 1787, for example the challenge was "Lachine" and the answer was "Quebec."

In 1795, three years after he joined the firm of Todd, McGill as partner, Andrew McGill replaced his brother permanently in the Fire Club; James evidently thought it was an important undertaking, even though with increasing responsibilities elsewhere he was glad to be able to pass this particular obligation over to someone else. It is notable that the fire club was limited to fourteen members, and was a distinctly self-help organization in that members only undertook to assist one another. Perhaps the fact that their bags were marked "Fire Club No. 1" meant that they expected other neighbours to organize similar clubs.

Other activities undertaken on behalf of neighbours benefited a larger and more general public. In 1783 McGill and an associate named Hertel de Rouville were representatives of the Union Company in a contract signed before lawyer E.W. Gray with a father and son named Fisbach. The Fisbachs were to set up and maintain for ten years two public water pumps, one to be located near the Jesuits' Garden close to McGill's own house, the other on the parade opposite the Parish Church of Notre Dame.[7] The supply of fresh clean water in the city was a matter of great importance, and to assist in its provision was to benefit a whole neighbourhood. A similar undertaking was the construction of a turnpike, or toll road, from Montreal to Lachine. It was still necessary for goods destined for Upper Canada or the Great Lakes and the Indian trade to be disembarked at Montreal and carted overland to Lachine for shipment upriver. This was still the only way to pass the Lachine Rapids. The improvement and the maintenance of the cart track between Montreal and Lachine so that it could be used by light wagons and passenger vehicles was a great step forward. James McGill accepted nomination as a commissioner for the Lachine Turnpike in 1805.

It was as a member of the commission to dismantle the old city walls that McGill performed one of his most notable services for Montreal, the one longest commemorated, apart from his famous bequest. These walls had never been of much benefit and had proved negligible during the American attack of 1775, the population having long overflowed into suburbs to the east, north, and west. They and the accompanying "Watch Road" alongside occupied much valuable space, so it was decided in 1802 to take them down. Three men were named to a commission to superintend the work, McGill, Jean-Marie Mondelet, and John Richardson. Both his colleagues were well known to McGill. Mondelet was a young man who had become prominent in city affairs and had emerged among the Canadiens as one of their leaders. Two years later he was to be elected to the Legislative Assembly to continue that leadership on the wider stage. Richardson was a colourful, vigorous Scot, ten years younger than McGill, who had come to Montreal in 1787 by way of business interests in Albany and New York. He had quickly become a leading figure in Montreal merchant circles, including the fur trade, and with McGill and some others had tried in 1792 to establish the Canada Banking Company. The time was not ripe and the attempt failed, but Richardson was to succeed twenty-five years later with the incorporation of the Bank of Montreal. A man of immense energy, he inititiated many major projects for the improvement of life in the city and province.[8] It was he who had proposed the Montreal-Lachine turnpike commission on which McGill had served. Now he was helping to demolish the old city walls. But unlike McGill, Richardson never understood the Canadiens' resolve to preserve their identity, language, and laws; he frankly and constantly urged them to "become British," for their own great benefit and the good of the province. Perhaps that is why, when an amusing difference of opinion arose among the commissioners at the end of their work, the outcome was decided in McGill's favour. On the west side of the city, where previously there had been only a narrow lane, the disappearance of the walls had left room for a new broad street, which deserved a new name:

Before they widened it, it was called St Augustin St. Mr McGill called it McGill Street, and entered it as such on the deed of homologation. Mr Richardson contended, on the contrary, it should be called after him and did likewise on the deed. Mr Mondelet also put in his claim, arguing with equal justice that it should be known as Mondelet Street, and in his turn also entered it as such. It is hard to tell who decided the question between these three contestants, but the deed shows that Mr Richardson's and M. Mondelet's names were erased, and Mr McGill's allowed to remain.[9]

Perhaps McGill won the support of third parties because he was known as a moderate in comparison with the strong Canadien sympathies of Mondelet and the British partisanship of Richardson. At any rate, the street still bears McGill's name. Along the waterfront, however, Commissioners Street honours the work of all three men.

These were some of the many contributions James McGill made over the years, as citizen and magistrate, to the life of his city. He had already rendered notable service in helping to negotiate the terms of surrender to the American forces in 1775; he was to be called upon to play an even larger role in resisting and defeating a return attack by those same forces in 1812. But in the intervening decades his energy and talents drew him into the wider concerns of the province as a whole, and he began to participate more and more significantly in the administration of the country he knew and loved as Canada.

7 Serving the Province, 1778–92

In the years from 1783 to 1812 much of the character of Canada was determined for the next two centuries, and James McGill, while attending assiduously to his own business affairs and to the needs of his friends and neighbours, found time to take a leading part in many of the major developments of the period. It began with the signing of the Treaty of Paris, which ended the American War of Independence and formally recognized the emergence of the United States of America as a sovereign nation. As noted earlier, the important clauses for Canada[1] were those settling the boundaries between the province of Quebec and the United States, and while the lines drawn confirmed the worst fears of McGill and his fellow merchants, nevertheless the authorization of reciprocal trading rights across the new boundaries worked fairly well. McGill's confidence that in commercial activities Canadians would be well able to hold their own was in the event fully justified.[2] The more immediate concern of the Montreal merchants after 1783 was that, an important part of the Quebec Act of 1774 having now been rendered obsolete, it was all the more necessary to procure the abolition, or at least substantial modification, of the rest of the act. The main offences for which it had been held responsible were the reinstatement of French law rather than British in matters of property and civil rights, which deprived litigants of the option of trial by jury in civil courts, and the loss of the protection of the Habeas Corpus Act in criminal courts, a consequence assumed rather than enacted but nonetheless abusive. The act also, of course, failed to make provision for an elected legislative assembly, whereby the Province could have effected its own remedies.

The British merchants of Quebec City and Montreal had long been active on these matters even before the signing of the 1783 treaty. Through the committee that they had established in London, they petitioned in 1778 to secure the repeal of the injurious parts of the Quebec Act – and in particular to reintroduce to Canada trial by jury in civil cases and to reinstate English law in commercial actions. One of the signatories was McGill's partner, Isaac Todd.[3] In 1784 they renewed their pleas, emphasizing the need for a legislative assembly. This document was signed by an impressive 233 citizens in Quebec City and 246 in Montreal, and the second name in the Montreal list was that of James McGill. Carleton had left the province in 1778 and his successor as governor, General Haldimand, was strongly opposed to the idea of a legislative assembly. He argued that had the British government earlier acceded to this request, Quebec would have long since joined the other colonies in their revolution. He also disapproved of the notion of trial by jury and felt no great concern for commercial law. As a Swiss soldier of fortune who had made his way up through the ranks of the military, he had in fact no great reverence for things English. He advised the British government to ignore the petition. But the merchants were persistent. Even when habeas corpus and jury trials were restored in 1784 and 1785 respectively, the major grievance still remained. But since Haldimand's term of office ended shortly thereafter, hope was renewed that this last barrier might yet be surmounted.

However, the return of Guy Carleton in 1786 for a second term as governor general dampened rather than strengthened that hope. He had been one of the most powerful influences shaping the Quebec Act of 1774 and had been in favour both of restoring French law within the province and of denying a legislative assembly to its citizens – the very things the British merchants most deplored. Many of the merchants had for many years regarded their governor as their chief opponent.[4]

McGill however was ready to think more positively of Carleton. James had known him as a courageous leader under enemy attack, and thereafter Carleton had proved himself a stout defender of the province in a time of great peril. As governor general he had done much to facilitate trade, specifically the fur trade, and he had attempted to be fair, even conciliatory, to the Canadien population, for whom McGill personally had a great regard. In McGill's view, Carleton had shown himself one of the few members of the British autocracy to have a genuine interest in Canada and in its future as a British dependency. As for the demands for a legislative assembly, he understood Carleton's coolness towards the idea but had become convinced that, given the basis of the British constitution, such an institution would prove the best means of procuring a clear, generally accepted, and flexible system of provincial laws within which trade might prosper and social life flourish. After 1783, therefore, he strongly supported his fellow British merchants in their petitions for an assembly. Moreover, as G.P. Browne comments, Carleton's own views had moderated considerably: "Both [he] and Quebec had changed considerably during the eight years he had been away. For his part he had become much less sympathetic to, or perhaps more nervous about, the Canadians, and much more understanding, and respectful of, the British colonists."[5] So McGill was not alone in thinking that the province of Quebec, newly defined by the Treaty of Paris, situated in the uncertain world of a British empire shorn of its other American colonies, and having to accommodate itself to the presence and rivalry of the new United States of America, would probably have its best opportunity of making progress under a renewed Carleton administration rather than under some other unknown appointee. He was one of many prominent citizens who gladly and sincerely signed an address of welcome to the returning governor general.[6]

Carleton began immediately to acquaint himself with the present state of the country and its affairs. He established four committees to investigate and report upon the operation of the courts of justice; the state of the militia, the roads and communications; matters pertaining to population, agriculture and the settlement of the Crown lands; and the regulation of external and internal commerce and the organization of police. The committees were empowered to call witnesses, and the Montreal magistrates, James McGill among them, were ready to testify on a number of matters, especially before the committee enquiring into the administration of police. For example they are on record as having testified:

The want of a proper Goal [sic] for this District, has long been complained of ... but hitherto no remedy has been applied. The House which at present serves for a Goal consists of four very small Rooms, in which are frequently confined promiscuously Persons of Different Sexes, and for very different Degrees of Crimes; The unfortunate Debtor cannot have a Room to himself, nor can the Malefactor when preparing for another World be accomodated with a place of retirement to deprecate the wrath of the offended Deity. The insufficiency of the Goal in point of security occasions a Guard of Soldiers to be kept in the lower part of it, and even with that precaution, many atrocious offenders have escaped, insomuch that the Sheriff of the District has refused to confine Debtors, unless the Prosecutor agreed to take upon himself the Risk of an Escape. The Situation of this insufficient Goal heightens the Sufferings of those Persons whom the Laws doom to an Imprisonment, offends every Passenger [i.e., passer-by] in the Warm Season and is a Nuisance to the Neighbourhood, being without those Conveniences requisite to carry off the Filth accumulated by want of them.[7]

McGill, as a former commissioner for this noisome horror, no doubt spoke forcefully and warmly on the subject. Accepting to be appointed to such a responsibility could have been no small matter. Death was frequently the punishment for relatively minor crimes such as theft, and even imprisonment entailed – and was meant to entail – considerable suffering. McGill administered law in a frontier town with its own harsh mode of justice. But that did not mean that he and his fellow magistrates were oblivious to the need for improvements.

McGill was also invited to appear before Carleton's justice committee. He had on this occasion a great deal to say concerning the system of jurisprudence prevailing in the province at large. He spoke not as a member of a group but as an individual, and since his testimony was recorded verbatim, we get a clear picture of the man as well as his contentions. The committee recognized that its enquiry was in large measure a response to the merchants' petition of 1784 and began by asking McGill to comment on that document. He replied in part:

I was one of a Committee at this place [Montreal] in the month of November 1784 and for several months afterwards for carrying thro' a Petition to His Majesty and to both Houses of parliament praying for a change in the constitution of the Legislature of this Province [which consisted at this time solely of the governor general's Legislative Council] in which Petition was also represented: 'That the Petitioners trusted in full confidence that his Majesty would relieve them from the anarchy and confusion, which at present prevail in the Laws and Courts of Justice in the Province by which their real property [i.e., real estate and goods] is rendered insecure. Trade is clogged and that good faith, which ought and would subsist among the people, and which is the life and Support of Commerce is totally destroyed' – or words to that Effect.[8]

As McGill saw the situation, the prevailing "anarchy and confusion" in legal matters had two main causes, the capricious and unpredictable judgments rendered in the court by reason of confusion in the laws on which those judgments were based, and the ineffectiveness of the only law-making body in the province, the small, unelected governor general's council. This was, he said, the main reason for his support of the 1784 petition asking for the institution of a legislative assembly. When asked to comment on his experiences of the courts and their working, he replied: "During a residence by intervals in this place from the year 1766 until the year 1775, and a constant residence since the last period till this day, being 21 years in all, I do not recollect having had more than three Suits in Court, in one of which I was Plaintiff and the other two Defendant."[9]

He then described one of the cases in which he was defendant in considerable detail. He had agreed, he said, to act as executor of the estate and guardian of the eight children of his deceased friend John Porteous,[10] whose widow had also died, leaving them orphans indeed. A certain Lt Col John Campbell had a note of hand for one thousand pounds currency signed by Porteous and had demanded payment from the Porteous estate. McGill had refused payment, contending, first, that according to French law as introduced by the 1774 Quebec Act, the note was void because, while it read "for value received," it did not specify what that value was and second, that the plaintiff had not given proof that John Porteous had in fact received "the value" in question – he cited the recent instance in which Mr Dooie, "an Emminent Merchant of this town," had in a similar case concerning a note of hand been required to bring his clerk and his books into court to prove that he had in fact delivered the value referred to in the evidence. Before defending his case in court, McGill had taken what he regarded as the best available advice in Montreal and Quebec City. However, "not contented with [these] Opinions I applied for advice to Mr Wm Grant an eminent Barrister of London, who resided some years in this Province in that profession, and he gave it also as his Opinion, that by the french [sic] law introduced as already mentioned, into this province, the note was not, nor could be considered as, good and sufficient to recover upon. Having so much authority to warrant me, I proceeded to *defend* the Suit, the issue of which was unfavourable to my great surprise and distress."

What riled McGill particularly was that his first point was set aside by the judges, who cited in support of their opinion a statute from *English* law promulgated in the reign of Queen Anne. As for the reference to Mr Dooie's action, the judges ruled the cases were not analogous, "that many circumstances such as the Character of the parties, et cetera, might occasion different Opinions – or words to that Effect." Having drawn attention to still further anomalies in the conduct of the case, McGill argued that this instance alone amply illustrated that cases might be settled on French law, as according to the Quebec Act they should be, but they might also be decided by reference to English law; that there were no settled rules relating to witnesses and the giving of evidence; and that judges decided cases arbitrarily without reference to precedents and settled procedures. "This case proves in my Opinion that there is anarchy and confusion in the Courts of Justice and that the laws of the Country and the practice of the Courts are at variance."[11] McGill had presented a persuasive argument for an elected and effective legislative assembly, which alone could correct this deplorable state of affairs. In this matter he and his friends were eventually going to win the day.

Meanwhile, he received a more unusual assignment. He was appointed in 1787 to a commission to advise the governor general on the Province's response to the proposal that the Jesuit estates should be granted to General, now Lord, Amherst in acknowledgment of his services in the conquest of Canada. This was a matter of great concern to Canadiens in general and generated strong emotions. The Society of Jesus founded by Ignatius Loyola in 1534 had by the second half of the eighteenth century fallen into disrepute throughout the world. The order had been banished from Portugal and Spain, and in 1762 the Parlement of Paris ordered all its colleges closed and its estates confiscated. This was followed in 1764 by a royal decree dissolving the order throughout the French dominions. The final blow came in 1773 when the pope himself suppressed the Society worldwide. The British in Canada had behaved very circumspectly with regard to the Roman Catholic secular clergy and the communities of nuns and had taken their time to consider what should be done with regard to the male religious orders, such as the Sulpicians and the Recollects. But in the instance of the Jesuits they had felt free from the beginning of their rule to suppress the activities of the order, sequester its land holdings, and make free use of its buildings. In the instructions to Governor General Carleton in January 1775, the British authorities went further: specific orders were given that the Society should be dissolved, and that its estates and other possessions should be vested in the Crown.[12] Their argument was that the French Crown had taken the action and the British Crown had inherited the results. Many Canadiens felt strongly that since the bequests had been made to the Jesuits, whether by the French Crown or by private donors, for the purposes of education (that being the Jesuits' main function), the estates belonged morally and legally to the Canadien people as a whole. The emotions aroused by this issue were one of the earliest manifestations of Canadien nationalism.

The estates in question were very large, extending to nearly 800,000 arpents: taking into account varying values for the *perche* (rod), this could mean anywhere from 670,000 acres to a million. Since the land holdings were so great the Jesuits were presumed to be very wealthy, but because the lands were largely undeveloped forest, the order was in reality land rich but cash poor. Nevertheless there were many claimants, including the Roman Catholic bishop of Quebec, ready and eager to show that they were the rightful heirs to the potential riches. After much manoeuvring, Carleton appointed nine commissioners at the end of 1787 to advise him on the matter: Kenelm Chandler, Thomas Scott, John Coffin, Gabriel Elzéar Taschereau, Jean-Antoine Panet, George Lawes, Quinson de St Ours, J-B Hertel de Rouville, and James McGill. Chandler was the governor general's agent, the next five represented Quebec City interests, and the last three

Montreal interests. Their assignment was truly demanding: they had to determine *inter alia* the extent and value of the estates, the manner in which they had been acquired, and whether any of the private donors had continuing rights.[13]

The commission's enquiry was a long, drawn-out affair. It became apparent early in the proceedings that if Chandler was the governor general's agent, Taschereau and Panet were equally the agents of French Canadian interests opposed to the alienation of the estates from their original purposes, and opposed particularly to their falling into the hands of a British absentee landlord. Their main tactic was foot dragging and administrative delay. When Chandler "railroaded" (the word is Dalton's) a draft report through a meeting held at Quebec City in June 1789, Taschereau and Panet refused to sign on the grounds that they had not had sufficient time to study it, but also because the Montreal commissioners were not present at the meeting. When McGill and his colleagues received a copy of the proposed report, they too refused to sign for the same reason: they had not had sufficient time to study the document. They also pointed out that the commission's obligations had not been observed; no enquiry had been made, whether other persons, such as heirs of donors of properties to the Jesuits, had continuing rights in the disposition of the estates.

The remaining Quebec commissioners nevertheless decided to present their report to the governor general, but noting their failure either to complete the enquiry or to attain unanimity. They concluded that by "right of conquest" the estates had passed from the French Crown to the British and should be so held, but that the question whether the British Crown was free to bestow all or any part on a third party could not be answered until enquiry had been made into the claims of other interested parties. This left matters nicely in limbo: the estates belonged to the Crown, but could not be assigned to Lord Amherst.

It is interesting to note some further developments. The law officers advising Carleton went further than the commission and said both that the Crown had title to the estates, and that the king's grant of them to Amherst was in order and that the governor general should authorize the grant forthwith. But Carleton once again proved a good friend of Canadian interests. He sent all the papers for decision to London, but with a remarkable letter:

He pointed out that the prevailing sentiment in the country was that the Jesuits' estates ought not be be diverted from public uses. There were different opinions on these uses, he noted, but the general wish was that they might be applied to the great object of education. Some advocated that the estates be used to support religious instruction and missionaries among the Indians, and that their management be placed in the hands of the Roman Church. Others argued that they be used for for various purposes of the Church of England. But the most enlightened [here Carleton was surely disclosing his own preference] wished to see such parts as were not wanted by the government appropriated for the support of a university for teaching the liberal arts and sciences on a plan that would avoid every occasion for religious disputes by the exclusion of all theological tuition.[14]

This letter effectively closed the work of the commission and also put an end to Amherst's hopes of securing the estates for himself – though he continued to press his claims and finally secured in compensation a life pension voted by the British House of Commons. The hope that Quebec education might benefit from the estates had a considerably longer life and was not settled finally until 1888.[15]

For James McGill the whole episode had been most enlightening. He had had further experience of working amicably with Canadien colleagues like St Ours and de Rouville, he had met and worked with senior members of the governor general's advisory circle, and he had gained hands-on experience of provincial administrative procedures. He had also seen for himself in the activities of Taschereau and Panet the growing organized resistance among French Canadians to the anglicizing of Canadien institutions – a resistance with which he was soon to become more closely acquainted in other aspects of his expanding public activities. He observed with approval the governor general's personal role in the outcome of the commission and judged that Carleton truly had the interests of the whole province, not just one of its factions, deeply at heart. That realization strengthened his own commitment to his adopted country. Finally, McGill could begin to discern the shaping of a splendid ideal: that one day in Quebec, as Carleton had put it, there might be an educational institution "teaching the liberal arts and sciences on a plan that would avoid every occasion for religious disputes by the exclusion of all theological tuition." When we remember the sectarian nature of education in both England and Scotland at that time, this was a visionary notion indeed, but it was one that stayed in his mind. To help bring that about in Quebec, perhaps even in Montreal, would surely be doing something truly worthwhile.

Interest in the need for a public educational system was not new to McGill. A year before he settled permanently in Montreal, he had helped to draw up a petition – one of the many asking for an elected legislative assembly – that had included a recommendation that some form of public education should be established. To strengthen the case, the petitioners had drawn attention to the fact that some Roman Catholic priests had recently established a school of their own, "which is all the more alarming as it excludes all Protestant teachers of any science whatever."[16] Already the desirability of a school system neutral on the subject of religion and designed for the whole population was beginning to have wider appeal, and Carleton's dispatch was one more stage in a long process in which James was going to play his own important part.

The matters considered by the 1787 committees were so important and the difficulties in the way of amendment so numerous that it is not surprising that Carleton and his council were not able to effect many major changes. But the institution of various amendments of a minor nature hastened the ongoing process of regularizing and improving the patterns of communal life in the province. By his participation in these efforts McGill was among those who were nudging public affairs in the right direction.

Even while James was wrestling with the thorny questions of the Jesuit estates, another significant development was beginning to gather momentum across the seas. Back in January 1785 the Montreal merchants, McGill among them, proposed to their colleagues who organized the London end of the Canada trading venture that an alliance between themselves and the representatives of the loyalists "might prove one of the most effectual measures for obtaining our earnest desires."[17] These loyalists were former Americans who were fleeing or being driven out of the United States and who were settling in ever greater numbers in Upper Canada. The suggested alliance proved a fruitful idea. A scheme emerged in London to divide the Province of Quebec into two separate jurisdictions, to be called Lower and Upper Canada, so that the loyalists settling in Upper Canada might have freedom to arrange their affairs according to their own desires. They were accustomed to having their own legislatures and making their own laws. But if a province of Upper Canada were to be accorded such status, could a province of Lower Canada be provided with less? Even those Canadiens who had most strongly opposed the idea of a popularly elected assembly, the seigneurs and the clergy, saw the cogency of this consideration. Support for the proposal strengthened both in Quebec and London to the point where in 1791, Prime Minister William Pitt secured passage through the British Parliament of a new constitution for Quebec.

The act provided for the division of the province of Quebec into the two provinces, Lower and Upper Canada, and gave to each a government based "as far as circumstances shall permit" on the British constitution. It authorized the defining of electoral districts, the specifying of voter qualifications, and the election of a House of Legislative Assembly in each province. The rights conveyed by the British Habeas Corpus Act were accorded to both provinces, confirming what was already the case in Quebec, and other laws currently in force were to continue in both provinces unless the government of either wished to alter them. An appointed legislative council in each province would act as an upper house.[18]

Because of these provisions, English law could be proclaimed to exist forthwith in Upper Canada, while in Lower Canada remedies could be provided for the many petitions that had circulated in the past, seeing that the assembly would now have the power to pass such laws as the members themselves enacted. They would, for example, be able to retain French law in civil matters and English law in the administration of criminal justice and straighten out the confused points in commercial law according to their own desires. It was to take many decades before all the ambiguities were settled – even the civil law was not satisfactorily codified until 1866 – but the population in general and the British merchants of Lower Canada in particular could now feel that public affairs had been steered onto the right course. The division of Quebec meant that in Lower Canada the British merchants would remain for the present very much a minority, but it was thought that immigration from Britain and the United States would in time correct the imbalance. The advantages, it was believed, outweighed the disadvantages.[19] In the matter of the assembly, McGill and his friends had now obtained what they had long wanted.

However, for James McGill personally, the first result was that a new public responsibility presented itself. He was asked to stand as a candidate for election to the new Legislative Assembly as one of two members for the constituency of Montreal West. Buoyed by the fact that his business affairs had weathered the 1786 crisis and had resumed their prosperous expansion, he consented, was elected, and became a member of the first Parliament of Lower Canada for the years 1792–96. That same year he was named an alternate member of the governor general's Executive Council. He was becoming a very public person.

8 The New Parliament, 1792–1808

The first session of the new Legislative Assembly of Lower Canada was opened on 17 December 1792, with appropriate ceremonies. There was first a speech from the throne read by the lieutenant governor, Sir Alured Clarke, and then the reading of loyal addresses to the throne, and finally the House could get down to the business for which it had been created. It must have been a momentous occasion for all present, and especially for men like William Grant, McGill's first fur-trader employer in Canada, a member for Quebec City, and now a landed seigneur and notable political figure; McGill's colleague John Richardson, a former anti-American naval privateer turned fur trader and already known as a leading figure among the Montreal merchants; and other "British" members as they were still called, many of whom had worked for this occasion for more than twenty years. But for none was it a more important day than for James McGill himself, who had such high hopes of the new legislative body. He saw it as the one institution able to draw the diverse components of the province into a true community, all the parts working together for the common good.

But it was also a significant day for many Canadien members, who were determined to use the assembly to safeguard their language, their religion, and their law – in a word, their identity. Among them were men like Jean-Antoine Panet, Grant's fellow member from Quebec City, known to McGill from the Jesuit-estates commission; and Jean-Marie Mondelet, with whom he had worked on the commission to dismantle the walls of Montreal; Jean-Baptiste Durocher, his fellow representative for Montreal West; and Joseph Papineau, the Canadien leader, who was one of the county members. For them the House of Assembly was a new theatre in which they could play their former roles to a province-wide audience and, perhaps hardly less important, one providing a Green Room where they could get to know one another and agree upon their aims and strategies.

From the beginning, then, it was clear that there were to be two parties in the House and that both were prepared to politic to achieve their ends – and McGill had close personal relationships with members on both sides of the House. The first skirmish occurred over the primary business of electing a speaker. After the formalities had concluded it was decided to defer this election until the next sitting; McGill therefore proposed adjournment until the day after the morrow, presumably to give members time to discuss the matter among themselves informally. But J.A. Panet proposed adjournment only until the next day, and his amendment was passed by ten votes – there were in all fifty elected members. The next day the House duly reconvened and the election was the first order of business. Panet was promptly proposed as speaker. McGill then nominated William Grant, but this met with objection because Grant's election was being challenged on the grounds of alleged illegal electioneering practices. So Grant nominated James McGill "because he speaks both languages." Panet's name was then put to the vote, and although it was known he had no English, he was elected by the same ten-vote majority recorded the previous day. The Canadien members had effectively served notice that the "British" members would not, as they had rather naively imagined, be able to dominate the House by virtue of their economic and business experience. Similarly, when it came to the question of determining the language of debate and of the records, the tensions in the assembly quickly made themselves apparent.

James McGill was distressed by this unpropitious beginning; he had hoped that the spirit of cooperation he had known in Montreal between the "Old and New subjects of His Majesty," as the phrase went, would be manifested in the legislature also. He wrote about it to his friend John Askin:

Quebec 20 January 1793

Dear Askin I was favoured whilst at Montreal with your esteemed Letter of the 2^d of November and as there will probably be no other opportunity of addressing you than this express untill the Spring I cannot let it pass without dropping you a few lines in return. Your partiality to me I have long known and if I can discharge the duties of the public employments I have been raised to, equal to your wishes, I shall not be apprehensive of forfeiting the good opinion which others have the goodness to entertain of me. I can answer for my heart but the Head may be wrong at times.

Our Legislature met on the 17th ult^o and as you will no doubt see our newspapers I need not take up your time with repeating the Governors Speech, the addresses of the two Houses &^c but referr you for them to the Gazettes.

Hitherto our time has been taken up in framing Rules for proceeding to business so that no Law has yet been brought forward and we have a point to discuss which I fear will set us at variance, for the Canadian Members will have all civil Laws passed in the French Language & only a translation of them in English. You will readily suppose that no Englishman can agree that a small Province shall treat the mother Country with such disrespect; besides ever since the Conquest of the Country the Laws have been passed in English & not a word said about it, but it would seem that the French revolution & Mr Paines Book on the rights of man have turned peoples Heads, for it is well known that the Governor cannot, & that the Legislative Council will not, pass any Law whatever in any other Language than in English. So much for our politics here and as to matters of business I shall referr you to the House [i.e., Todd, McGill & Co.].

I beg my best Compliments may be made acceptable to Mrs Askin & your family & that you will believe me,

My dear Askin, Your affectionate Friend

James McGill[1]

This is a significant letter in many ways. First, a minor but interesting point: it was dispatched on 20 January and was received on 11 March. How did it get from Quebec City to Detroit in the midst of winter in fifty days? From the time of the French regime there had been a road from Quebec to Montreal; it had more recently been improved with post-houses and inns but still left much to be desired. After Montreal there was a track to Cornwall and then only paths in the wilderness. Probably McGill's letter was included with military mail making its way from post to post by horse and sleigh, or by runners on snowshoes. It is a vivid reminder of the difficulties of early Canadian communications. Secondly, it is noticeable that by now McGill has no hesitation in thinking of himself and his British friends as "English." His tombstone, reflecting no doubt his own practices, was to describe him as "a native of Glasgow, North Britain." His identification with the British Crown and empire had by this time fully replaced any earlier loyalties, though emotional ties to Scotland and "his ain folk" remained very strong. Thirdly, McGill's reply suggests that Askin had written to congratulate him on his election to the legislature and had made some such remark as "how fortunate Lower Canada is to have such a man as you to serve its public business." McGill acknowledges with no false modesty the good standing he has achieved in general opinion, but tempers his self-approbation with the revealing phrase "the duties of the public employments I have been raised to": service to the community, whether of the city or the province, has indeed conferred on him dignities, but it has also conferred heavy duties and responsibilities. He goes on to admit he may make mistakes, but reaffirms his sincere intention to seek the good of his country: the head may be wrong at times, he allows, but "I can answer for my heart." It is the self-judgment of an honest man.

The business of language in the legislature took many weeks to settle. Finally it was agreed that "no motion shall be debated or put, unless the same be in writing and seconded. When a motion is seconded, it shall be read in English and in French by the speaker, if he is master of both languages."[2] If he were not, he could read the motion in his own language, and the clerk of the House would read it in the other. As for the records: "Resolved, this house shall keep its journal in two registers, in one of which the proceedings of the House shall be wrote in the French language, with a translation of the motions originally made in the English language; and in the other shall be entered the proceedings of the House and the motions in the English language, with a translation of the motions originally made in the French language."[3] So the bilingual pattern was set, cumbersome but, as this first session had proved, vitally necessary.

THE

PROVINCIAL STATUTES

OF

LOWER-CANADA.

Anno Regni GEORGII III. Tricefimo Tertio.

HIS EXCELLENCY THE RIGHT HONORABLE

GUY LORD DORCHESTER GOVERNOR.

'AT the Provincial Parliament, begun and holden at *Quebec*, the Seventeenth day
' of December, *Anno Domini*, One thoufand feven hundred and ninety-two, in the
' thirty-third year of the Reign of our Sovereign Lord G E O R G E the Third, by
' the Grace of G O D, of *Great-Britain*, *France and Ireland*, K I N G, Defender of the
' faith, &c.

' Being the firft Seffion of the firft Provincial Parliament of LOWER-CANADA.'

C A P.   I.

An ACT to prevent the bringing of GUN-POWDER in Ships or other Veffels into the Harbour of *Montreal*, and to guard againft the carelefs Tranf-
porting of the fame into the *Powder-Magazines*.

Preamble.

WHEREAS the bringing of Gun-Powder on board of Ships or other Veffels into the
Harbour of *Montreal*, is attended with great rifk and danger to the town and alarming to the Inhabitants thereof, by reafon of the proximity of the Buildings to the Harbour
or ufual place of unloading at the market Gate : And whereas the landing of Gun-Powder
from on board of Ships or other Veffels, and the Carting thereof into the Powder Ma-
gazines may, if not carefully attended to, be productive of the moft fatal effects : Be
it therefore enacted by the King's moft Excellent Majefty by and with the Advice
and Confent of the Legiflative Council and the Affembly of *Lower-Canada*, confli-
tuted and affembled by virtue of and under the Authority of an Act paffed in
the Parliament of Great Britain intituled " *An Act to repeal certain parts of an act*
" *paffed in the fourteenth Year of His Majefty's Reign*" intituled " *An Act for making more*
No Veffel to en- " *effectual Provifion for the Government of the Province of Quebec in North America and*
ter the Harbour " *to make further Provifion for the Government of the faid Province.*" That from and
of Montreal with after the publication of this Act, it fhall not be lawful for the Mafter or Maf-
more than five ters of any Ship or other Veffel to enter into the Harbour of *Montreal*, which fhall
pounds of Gun- be confidered for this purpofe to extend to the Channel on the off-fide of the little
Powder under pe- Ifland near to the Town, with more than five pounds of Gun-Powder on board any
nalty of ten fuch Ship or other Veffel, under the penalty of ten pounds current money of this
pounds. Province : Provided always that it fhall be lawful to all and every Mafter or Maf-
Permiffion to un- ters of Ships or other Veffels on arriving at the Crofs or Foot of the current near to the
load Gun-Powder Town of *Montreal*, there to unload and land the Gun-Powder he or they fhall have on
at the Crofs near board of their refpective Ships or other Veffels.
Montreal.
II.

The first Act of the Legislature was proposed by James McGill.

James McGill continued to play a leading role in the provincial
legislature. He had the honour of proposing the first bill to be accepted and enacted: an ordinance forbidding ships laden with
gunpowder from docking in Montreal harbour and also regulating
the transport of powder to the magazine on St Helen's Island. In
1793 his alternate membership on the governor general's Executive Council was changed to permanent status and he became the
Honourable James McGill. He was also named the member who
would convey the council's communications to the lower house,
and this was regarded as an office of distinction and influence. He

Le premier Acte de la législature était proposé par James McGill.

served in three provincial parliaments, those of 1792–96, 1800–04, and 1804–08 (he declined nomination in 1796), and was an active and constructive member.[4] He participated, for example, in legislation concerning the repair of roads in and around Montreal, construction of a road to Upper Canada, the siting and construction of city jails in Montreal and Quebec City, the regulation of fishing in the waters off the Gaspé coast, the importation of goods such as wampum and tobacco leaf by land or inland waters, the care of foundlings and the insane, and many other similarly diverse matters. One item that catches the eye is his appointment to a committee to translate into French a message from the lieutenant governor; he was often called upon "to examine and correct" the records of the House in either language, so his abilities in English and French must have been considerable and widely recognized.

But even so, he often found the business of the assembly fatiguing and burdensome, and he felt deeply the long separation from home. He wrote again to Askin in January 1794: "Tomorrow I propose setting out to Quebec, where I fancy my Stay will be protracted until April if not to May. If such Employments confer honor, they are dearly paid for by those who have families."[5]

One contentious issue was the provision of a system of public education. The first petition McGill had ever signed, back in 1774, had emphasized the urgency of the matter, and the same concern had been raised many times among his associates and friends during the intervening years. When Carleton instituted his committees in 1787 to review the state of the province, the one dealing with education was probably the most sensitive. It was chaired by Chief Justice William Smith. A loyalist and former New England Tory, he had little feeling for Canadien susceptibilities, and his committee produced in 1789 the outline of a highly centralized system that provided for an elementary school in each village, a secondary school in each county, and a "secular college" to serve the needs of both anglophones and francophones. At every level education was to be free of all charges. But the scheme recognized no place for the Church, either Catholic or Protestant, since the governor general was to nominate all personnel from the governing board down to individual teachers. Consequently, the report was condemned out of hand by the Roman Catholic bishop of Quebec, a dictum that effectively put an end to all Canadien cooperation and to the report's practicality.

The next move came from Jacob Mountain, the new government-appointed Anglican bishop of Quebec. He arrived in 1793 and at once began urging the government in London and the governor general in Canada to become active in this matter of public education. The business hung fire for several years, because Carleton and his successor were sensitive to Canadien feelings, but when Sir Robert Milnes arrived as governor in 1799, he listened sympathetically to Mountain and quickly placed a memorandum from the bishop before the Executive Council. Mountain argued the need for "a good Grammar School" in the province, to be staffed by "able Masters from England" and paid for by the government. He went on to plead the cause of elementary education:

It is well known that the lower orders of the people in this Province are for the most part deplorably ignorant; that the very slender portion of instruction which their children obtain is almost entirely confined, amongst those who do not live in the Towns, to the girls alone; and more especially, it is notorious that they have hitherto made no progress towards the attainment of the language of the country under which government they have the happiness to live. This total ignorance of the English language on the part of the Canadians draws a distinct line of demarcation between them and his Majesty's British subjects in this Province, injurious to the welfare and happiness of both; and continues to divide into separate peoples those, who by their situation, their common interests and their equal participation of the same laws and the same form of Government, should naturally form but one.[6]

His solution, of course, was that the Canadiens should learn English, and he proposed that schoolmasters resident in the countryside should be paid by the government to teach children the language free; for a small fee they would also teach pupils writing and arithmetic.

This unashamedly anglicizing memorandum would not have got past Carleton, but it appealed to the less-experienced Milnes, and it also won the approbation of the colonial secretary in London. Milnes was encouraged to attempt the implementation of the bishop's proposals and the colonial secretary went so far as to hint that some Crown lands might be made available to provide financial support. As a result, a bill entitled "An Act for the Establishment of Free Schools in this Province" was prepared and presented to the Legislative Assembly of Lower Canada.

It has been said that the Canadien majority in the legislature had not been alerted to the significance of this bill and that even the clergy "were slumbering," so that it slipped through more or less unnoticed. But the facts are that there was considerable debate and indeed determined opposition.[7] The bill was discussed at length in a Committee of the Whole House on 2 March, but on the same day François-Joseph Perrault, himself a member of the original drafting committee, sought leave to introduce another bill "to establish public schools in the parishes of Lower Canada." Unfortunately no copy has survived but obviously it differed significantly from the administration's bill, especially in putting the proposed schools under the control of parish councils – that is, under the control of the Church. The clear intention was to kill the earlier bill and substitute this new one, but after prolonged discussion the motion was defeated by sixteen votes to seven, and the original bill passed.

But the fight was not yet over. The Legislative Council reviewed the bill and returned it to the House with no less than eighteen amendments. Presumably they were of a minor procedural nature, for Judge Debonne proposed that they be accepted *en bloc.* But this gave the opponents of the bill one last chance to kill it. Pierre-Stanislas Bédard, one of the most militant of the Canadien majority, proposed an amendment whereby the vote would be deferred until 1 August, when the House would not be sitting, so that no vote could take place and the bill would die. The motion was defeated but only by eleven votes to nine. The amendments were then proposed and passed *en bloc,* and the bill went back to the Legislative Council and so to the lieutenant governor for royal assent. Instead of being deferred "to await His Majesty's pleasure," as acts of the legislature often were, this measure received assent on 7 April 1801: but to say that Quebec's first education act slipped past while the Canadien party and the clergy slumbered is not correct.

James McGill was of course a member of the House while this bill, by which he and his associates had set such great store, was being debated. More than once its fate had trembled on such narrow majorities that every vote counted. One would therefore expect to find that McGill was well to the fore, voting and contending for its passage. But a scrutiny of the records reveals that during this crucial period McGill was notably absent from the assembly. Mention was made in the preface of the three survivors of the long line of McGill's calendar diaries. By great good fortune one of them is for the year 1801, and in McGill's crabbed handwriting, we find the explanation:

January, 1801. Set out from Montreal the 6th, arrived at quebec [sic] on the 9th in the Evening, but not very well – refrained from going to House of Assembly until the 14th, having taken Physic twice and apparently pretty well, yet a cough continued – on the 29th the Gout attacked me severely in the left Leg and kept me to my room until 23rd February, having had much fever but no great degree of Gouty Pain. February, 1801. About the 22nd was able to go down Stairs and on the 24th to take an airing in the Curicle and have continued mending yet not perfectly well nor free from Gout on the 28th of the month –

March 1801. from 1–8th continued mending but still not capable of pulling on Shoes and the left hand somewhat swoln [sic]. I dine with the Governor and wish it may not be early – for three days the weather moist and wind N. Easterly which has prevented me from riding out; from Montreal, Letters say great appearance of Spring.[8]

The education bill touched McGill's interests closely and was to mean a great deal for his future plans, yet ironically, while it was being debated, he was literally *hors de combat*. He was confined to his Quebec lodgings, heartily wishing he was comfortably at home in the solicitous care of Mme McGill and "the amiable Miss Porteous."

In the months and years that followed, it must have seemed that the passage of the act had been of no value, for the steadfast refusal of the Canadien clergy to cooperate in its implementation consigned it to a dusty pigeon-hole. The act had sanctioned the establishment of the Royal Institution for the Advancement of Learning, and the essential first step was for the lieutenant governor to name the members of its governing board – but no Roman Catholics would serve, and to name only Protestants would arouse antagonism. Successive administrators were content to let the matter lie.

But at least in Montreal the cause of English education did not languish altogether. Already in 1796, the city's first public library had been organized. It was a joint-stock operation, offering up to 120 participants shares at £10 apiece. James McGill was one of the directors. Three years later, a young schoolteacher from Scotland named Alexander Skakel was invited to set up school in the city, and he did so in Little St James Street in 1799. It was called the "Classical and Mathematical School" – aptly named, for as usual at that time the description fairly well covered the whole curriculum. James McGill took a particular interest in this school because the schoolmaster was also exploring "natural philosophy," or, as we should say, science. For this he needed instruments, particularly lenses, telescopes, microscopes, and other optical apparatus. He was also interested in the new subjects of electricity, galvanism, and magnetism and he conducted experiments in chemistry, holding evening lectures for interested adults. His fellow citizens, including James McGill, were ready to encourage these activities, and when Skakel let it be known that he needed more instruments than he could afford, generous citizens contributed to a fund to which he could have recourse.[9] McGill subscribed generously to Skakel's apparatus fund and was invited to act as one of three trustees to administer it.[10] This pioneering contribution to the cultural and intellectual life of Montreal was unique and reinforced the public-minded merchant's growing interest in giving to Montreal what his own alma mater had given to Glasgow and to him.

Meanwhile, McGill completed his elected term but, as noted earlier, declined renomination in 1796. He needed to attend to his own affairs and especially those of his family and dependents. But in 1800 and 1804 he was again elected, serving in all for twelve years as a member of the Legislative Assembly of Lower Canada. By 1808, however, relations between Britain and the United States were fast deteriorating and he judged he should turn his attention once again to the military defence of his city. He had long been an officer of the militia; from now on this responsibility must have the prior claim.

But before entering upon the last and most remarkable chapter of his story, we look more closely at James McGill the man in his society, his home, and his personal relationships.

9 The Honourable James McGill, 1775–1811

In his younger career, James McGill was primarily a good example of the eighteenth-century merchant. His programs and his values were those of the entrepreneur, a role he saw as having its own practices, standards, and obligations. He viewed himself and his fellow merchants very much as his father and his grandfather had viewed their craft, and though his "guild" was less highly organized, it constituted for the more responsible members such as himself a valid community of interests and practices. Long before it was inaugurated, McGill was a loyal member of the Montreal Chamber of Commerce.[1]

Consequently, McGill's word was his bond, his goal was to seek profits, his trade was to take risks. As he once told John Askin in the active days of his career, a merchant does not tie up capital in land – he ventures it in the market. In his later career, when he had achieved sufficient financial success, he did indeed begin to acquire land since it was the only means available in the preindustrial age of conserving gains won in the marketplace. And certainly he had gains; he was a remarkably successful member of the merchant community. He was said in his last days to be the richest man in Canada, but that was more of a soubriquet than a factual evaluation. Because we do not have his financial records, we cannot trace the details of his accumulation of wealth – to begin to draw together any kind of balance sheet from the James and Andrew McGill Company day book, one would need to have the numbered accounts to which it refers. It is highly likely his wealth was much exaggerated. Alexander Henry (for what his testimony is worth) said that one of his two residual heirs, Francis Desrivières, would receive some $60,000, which would point to a total estate of about $140,000 to $150,000, but whether that included land values (some titles being rather dubious and prices often quite arbitrary) is uncertain.

The money was made in merchandizing, and here James McGill accepted established practices; indeed, as regards the fur trade he had no other choice, but even in general merchandizing there is no sign that he wished to bring in changes. Employees' wages were miserably low, and, as shown for example in the contract with Pierre Picotte, the voyageurs' financial rewards were niggardly in the extreme. Eighteenth-century life did not provide many opportunities for upward mobility. The merchant risked his money and either made or failed; the worker gave his labour and subsisted on a pittance. McGill did not question that; he was a man of the eighteenth century who lingered into the nineteenth, but he was certainly not a twentieth-century social reformer. As his comment on Paine's book suggested even within the accepted practices of his day he was a Tory rather than a democrat.

It was the same in his dealings with the native peoples. He accepted unquestioningly the habits of the established trade. It is most unlikely that he ever considered that he was taking part in a clash of cultures, or that his exchange of guns for furs was undermining a whole way of life, or that his merchandise of blankets and metal goods was making the native dependent upon the white man – or even, as was already obvious to some at least, that gifts of firewater were demoralizing an ancient and proud people. The tides of history were flowing, and James McGill was one of those being carried along with them.

In matters of religion, James McGill and his "enlightened" century seem to have agreed very well. He had left Scotland too young to have become embroiled in the internal strife of his Presbyterian heritage (the "First Secession Church of Scotland" was formed by Ebenezer Erskine the year that James was born) and whatever formal habits he may have developed while in the predominantly Anglican Carolinas, he found when he arrived in Montreal a situation much to his liking. There was only one Protestant congregation, ministered by a Swiss pastor, David Delisle, supposedly bilingual but in fact markedly deficient in English. Pastor Delisle therefore read the services as prescribed in the Book of Common Prayer, but any teaching was naturally in the Calvinist Reformed tradition of his homeland and so very akin to what McGill was accustomed to from his Presbyterian upbringing. When the congregation received English clergy and became distinctively Anglican under the name Christ Church, McGill saw no reason to discontinue his association and continued to rent his pew there. But when in 1786 Scottish merchants organized the St Gabriel Street Presbyterian congregation he subscribed ten guineas to the building fund and when the new edifice was opened, he took a pew in that church also. When Christ Church decided to erect a new parish church, later to become a cathedral, he again subscribed generously. In 1796 the Province appointed a commission to oversee the repair and maintenance of the Catholic churches in the Montreal region, and McGill consented to serve as the one Protestant member. Clearly, in matters of religion, James McGill took St Paul's admonition to heart – he was "all things to all men." He respected the place of religion in communal life and conformed to its practices – he and Mrs McGill stood as godparents at several christenings in the Christ Church congregation – but he was moved by no religious fervours of his own.[2] He acknowledged God as the Great Architect of creation; he accepted the place of a Prime Mover in a Newtonian universe, and he observed the outward conventions – but he has left no hint of any personal convictions. When he came to write his will, it was as a purely secular document.

On the other hand, it is also true that among his own people McGill had an unusually well-developed sense of communal obligation and devoted himself more and more to the performance of public duties. The persona of officeholder grew steadily, and the career of merchant decreased accordingly. Finally, during his last two years his public obligations took over, and he devoted all his time and energy to them, knowing that he had been called to fulfil, on behalf of his city and country, a role that he neither could nor wanted to refuse.

Where we would dearly welcome more information is on his daily relationships with those nearest to him. We know that he was a reserved man, not given to easy social intercourse but capable of deep affections – for Mrs McGill, for example, and for his adopted daughter, "the amiable Miss Porteous," and for his friend and partner, Isaac Todd. He also seems to have had a particular sensitivity to young people. All his life he was providing for them or taking care of them, as often as not on behalf of one or other of his friends. Childless himself, there was something of the pied piper about him.

The procession of young charges began in 1776 when James married Charlotte Desrivières and became stepfather to her two sons, François Amable and Thomas Hippolyte. As noted earlier, they were twelve and seven years old when McGill married their mother; her brother-in-law Hippolyte Desrivières had legal responsibility for them, but he died while they were still young. They lived with their mother in McGill's home, and he early established cordial relations with them. In later life, he treated François, or Francis as he was often called, very much as his heir. When, for example, McGill attended dinners at the Frobisher mansion, Francis sometimes accompanied him as a son might accompany his father.[3] Moreover, he followed James into a business career, which increased the strength of the bond between them. He became a junior partner in the Todd, McGill Company and in its successor, the James and Andrew McGill Company. Towards the end of McGill's life, Francis was named one of the three residuary heirs to the McGill fortune, and as a sign of particular regard Francis was to receive James' gold watch. The ties were never so close with the younger boy; he chose a military career, and James secured a commission for him in the sixtieth (Royal American) Regiment, but sadly he died in a foolish duel. However, he left a son, James McGill Guy Trottier Desrivières, in whom McGill, his adoptive grandfather, took a close interest. He provided for his upbringing and education, and named him also as a residuary heir.

Three years after his marriage another young person came to live in the hospitable McGill household. In 1779 John Askin asked James and more particularly Madame McGill to receive his daughter Madelaine into their home. She was the second child of Askin's liaison with his Indian spouse, and he clearly thought a frontier upbringing would not would fit her for a suitable marriage. She came into Madame McGill's care to receive training in household management and an education proper for a young girl of good family. She stayed seven years, long enough to establish familial

James McGill. Artist John Gilroy, 1959.

relationships, and in 1786 McGill could write to his friend: "Your daughter Madelaine is in perfect health and when a proper opportunity offers, It is my intention to fulfil Mrs Askin's and your wishes by sending her up, and I am pretty certain you will find her bien entendu dans le menage insomuch that I fancy you will not keep her many years Mademoiselle. I expect Todd from England early and as there will be little to do here, he may probably pay you a visit, taking Madelaine with him."[4]

McGill's prophecy was confirmed when the young woman married Dr Robert Richardson, a surgeon in the British army.[5] Fifteen years after she had left his home, McGill still remembered Madelaine with affection and in his will made her a bequest of £250 – further testimony to the depth and persistence of his affectionate relationships. And then there are the references in the J. and A. McGill 1798 financial journal to the "board and education of little A.Todd," and in the 1805 letter to "the little girls Agnes and Jane" and "the little Boy" whose health gave rise to much anxiety[6] – probably, as commented earlier, some of Isaac Todd's responsibilities conveniently left in McGill's hospitable care.

An ongoing obligation arose from the death of John Porteous, the fur-trading friend who died in 1782, leaving a widow and eight children on whose behalf McGill had defended the lawsuit. James undertook the burial of his friend, purchasing the plot in the old Protestant cemetery in which he was interred. A ninth child, a girl, was born posthumously. McGill and his wife accepted to stand as godparents at the child's christening; she was named Charlotte after Mrs McGill. But then the mother died also, so the McGills took their godchild into their own home and brought her up, with Madelaine Askin's help, as their daughter. Madelaine was particularly attached to "l'enfant chéri." McGill acted as executor for the estate of his deceased friend and also as "tutor" to the orphans. Under the French law of Quebec, the person or persons so named were *in loco parentis*, and while it is to be presumed that the older girls were boarded in McGill's home for some years, the youngest lived her whole life there. In either case, James watched over the girls' welfare and when two of them became of marriageable age he mentioned in a letter to Askin that he was aware of the need to make suitable matches for them, and doubtless to provide modest dowries, out of the Porteous estate or from his own resources.[7] McGill's fatherly concern for these girls is one of many examples of his unusual kindness and generosity within his own limited circle.

The youngest Porteous daughter, however, was from the beginning in a different relationship. Over the years, she endeared herself greatly to her adoptive parents and gave them much pleasure. Madame McGill, it will be remembered, had lost two little girls of her own before she married James, and Charlotte Porteous helped to fill an unhappy void in her life. In McGill's will, Charlotte was named as the third of the residuary heirs, but as we shall hear, sadly, she did not live to inherit.

There were also sons in the Porteous family and we know that James helped at least one of them, a young man named John after his father, in some business affairs that did not turn out well. McGill lost money in this venture and evidently agreed with the general opinion that John had not behaved well in the affair, for in his will he left £750 to each of two other Porteous brothers but to John £250 only.[8] However, his remembering the sons at all, some thirty years after their father's death, is remarkable evidence of his continuing sense of responsibility for this orphan family.

These same characteristics in personal relationships reveal themselves even more clearly in his dealings with his long-time friend John Askin. Askin was located first at Mackinac and after 1780 at Detroit. Sometime after 1796, when Detroit was finally handed over to the Americans, he moved across the river to Sandwich, Windsor, in order to remain Canadian. In all three locations he was a longtime associate of the Todd, McGill Company and later of the James and Andrew McGill Company. But he was constantly in debt to his Montreal suppliers. From time to time James McGill would chide Askin, urging him to pay off the mounting obligation, but neither firm ever cut off his supplies. Askin's weakness was that he would buy great tracts of land, often from Indians, so that his titles were precarious. Much of the land was on what became the American side of the new frontier, and many of his titles were disallowed when the new authorities took control. But Askin had used these holdings to pay off his Montreal debts, and so Todd, McGill and Company were the eventual heavy losers. However in 1786 the particular crisis in the affairs of the Todd, McGill Company caused James to write to Askin with more than usual urgency:

Montreal 12 April 1786

Dear Askin   I must not let the first oppertunity [*sic*] of the Spring slip over without my personal Respects & I hope they will find you well in your health & a fair prospect of plentiful Returns from the Indian Country.

The House having wrote you on business, leaves me nothing further to say on that head than to conjure you by every tie of friendship to leave no stone unturned in order to make remittances, for on this Summer depends our own existence as men of Character & Credit. The very scanty payments we made last year, has left us indebted with our friends in England so largely that Todd writes me he was under the necessity of relinquishing every Scheme of business except the shipping a few dry Goods & some Rum, being afraid to run further in debt & perhaps even meet with a refusal of further Credit. This situation I need not tell you the cause, least [i.e., lest] it should have an appearance of reproach; your own feelings will dictate what must be mine. I have no occasion to say more, than that I depend confidently on you acting in consequence. Do not suppose that, because I have been complaining for years past, the necessity is not greater than it was; the case is much altered – a bad trade here, a scarcity of money & near double the sum owing us from above [i.e., from up country]; but why should I detain you with this exposition of affairs, knowing that you will leave nothing undone that may be in your power to accomplish.[9]

The crisis was so severe that when Todd returned from England that spring, McGill himself travelled back with him to London in the fall to continue efforts to allay the fears of their London creditors. As we have seen, he accomplished his purpose. Todd, McGill weathered the storm and continued healthily until the James and Andrew McGill Company took over its business; but the delicacy of McGill's language as he makes his appeal to Askin while refraining from either blame or reproach is indeed remarkable. By 1792 Askin's debt had not decreased and McGill wrote again, rather more sternly:

Montreal 24 January 1792

Dear Sir   The House as wrote you this day handing acc[ts] Current from which it appears that the Balance will be on the 10th of April next £20,217 exclusive of any Rum you may have taken to account. Sensible that the Interest of so large a Balance must for ever keep you back, & whatever the sum may be which you shall finaly [sic] fall short being to revert against the late firm of Todd & McGill, I wish much to put matters on such footing after the 10th of April as may give you a fair chance of unburthening yourself, more especialy [sic] as our present House is to be somewhat altered by the introduction of my Brother Andrew as a Partner; and as the [new] House are to benefit by the transactions they are to have with you, it is but just they should run the risk of any eventual loss or disappointment, without the guarantee of Todd & McGill as has hitherto been the Case.

In order to Effect these purposes I propose that you shall pay off so much of your account next Season as will leave the balance £15,000 net and this Sum I shall withdraw from the Books of the present concern [i.e., James and Andrew McGill] altogether, giving you five years [to pay it back] without Interest, reserving only to go towards payment of it annualy [sic] so much as you may remitt more than your future account may come to with our new House.[10]

Certainly a stern letter, but one proposing an exceedingly generous arrangement that might, one would expect, have bestirred Askin to prevent any further increase in his indebtedness. But only two years later James is writing once more:

Montreal 10 January 1794

Dear Askin   I am your Debtor for more Letters than used to be the Case but as most of them are on business & chiefly answered by me from the House I hope you will excuse me if I have not written you oftener personaly [sic].

Now that the business of the year appears closed, it is most painful to observe that your remittances of this Season are far short of the Goods sent you. In 1793 the former [year] was much worse, in so much that in the two years it appears to me that you fall short nearly if not fully £4000 Currency exclusive of accumulating Interest. Such heavy disappointment have brought your Friend Todd & me into a most unpleasant situation & what is finaly [sic] to be the result I know not, for we must take upon ourselves whatever you may fall short to the Company. If therefore you have for us that regard & friendship which I never doubted, you will assuredly see the necessity of making every possible exertion to prevent us from being the greatest Sufferers that can probably be instanced in Trade to your part of the world. Unwilling to wound your feelings further I shall not add on this very painful Subject.

Again very restrained language, and it is in keeping that the sub-
scription reads, "I beg of you to assure Mrs Askin and your family
of Mrs McGill's and my best respects and believe me, Dear Askin,
Your Sincere Friend, James McGill."[11] Sincere friend indeed. There
is little evidence that Askin ever did set the books straight, except
by more transfers of land at his own valuation, most of which was
lost when the new frontiers were enforced. In Windsor Askin was
able to acquire two government posts, the income from which enabled him to retrieve his personal fortunes and end his days in
comfort and comparative affluence. But at least he was not unap-
preciative of his benefactor's long-suffering kindness:

> Near Sandwich, April 23^{d} 1806
> My Dear sir   Your most frindly [sic] private Letter of the 10th February
> reached me on the 11th Inst; Surely I must be the most ungratefull of men
> if I did not feel for your Person & Interest all the concern due by a person
> to his greatest Benefactor, was it not for your, & Our most worthy Frind
> Mr Todds lenity & generosity formerly and yours laterly [sic], I must long
> since have seen Myself & Family in real want, nor have you been sparing
> in Action only not to hurt my Character & feelings but also in words, and
> I have often declared Publicly and will whilst I live, that in all my Trans-
> actions with Mr Todd & you formerly, nor your House laterly, did I Ever
> receive a harsh nor Unfrindy line from you, even when I owed you such
> large Sums, as you knew never could be discharged; Indeed had you
> wrote me in the Stile, Other Houses have to their Debtors, I have every
> reason in the world to believe, from what I know of my too tender feel-
> ings, that I would many years Ago have been out of the reach of Corri-
> sponding with any one this side of the Grave. This is verry weak I know,
> but man did not make himself. I have courage & Philosophy in many
> cases, but the loss of old Frinds or their Frinship Overcomes me. Well
> must Mr Todd & you have know my Natural disposition, to have treated
> me with the tenderness you have done; I hope & believe you will have
> your reward in a better world.[12]

He then excuses himself for having perhaps gone too far in this
letter in "Urging you to take 20 Lots and discharge me from the
Debt due to your present House." Dear Askin! He never changed.
It is characteristic of this friendship that when after 1796 Askin decided to relocate in Windsor on the Canadian side of the border, it
was Todd, McGill Company that gave him back some lands of
good title on which to set up his new estate.

It is something of a mystery how McGill managed to absorb these immense losses and still remain not merely solvent but affluent. In a letter to Askin written in 1806, Alexander Henry mentions that McGill is going up to Mackinac to settle with a trader called "Dixon" who owes him £40,000 currency, and McGill is afraid he will lose "the greatest part."[13] There must have been a tremendous mark-up of goods between London and Montreal and again between Montreal and the up-country destinations to provide for bad debts, so perhaps these sums represent in large part loss of anticipated profits rather than loss of monies expended.[14]

After all, James McGill was a merchant and keen and shrewd in his business affairs. It will be recalled that one administrator had complained of the "rapacity" of Todd, McGill Company. But when in 1805, long after Detroit had become American, the settlement there was swept by a fire that destroyed every building except one, McGill was foremost in organizing a relief fund in Montreal for the victims of the disaster. He worked hard to build up a large fortune, but he knew how to be generous with it.

Seeing that so much is known about McGill's relations with Askin (solely because Askin kept the correspondence), it is somewhat mortifying to realize how little we know about James' relations with his own family, and especially with his brothers John and Andrew. What little information there is was conveyed in the earlier discussion of their father's financial difficulties in 1773–74. Any other information about the brothers comes from their wills. John's testament, dictated to a notary in November 1797, was composed shortly before his death. Small legacies were specified for his "loving Sister Margaret, Spinster, of Glasgow," for his uncle Ninian, rather surprisingly described as "Gentleman" (which may be the notary's way of saying the uncle had no known occupation), for his apprentice-clerk, and for servants. But all John's household effects, furniture, linen, and the like were left to Madame McGill, James' wife; and £850 was left in trust to James to be used "for the use and behoof" of Margaret and Charlotte Porteous and of James McGill Desrivières, Madame McGill's grandson. The rest of the estate was to be divided two thirds to his brother James and one third to his brother Andrew.[15] It is clear that in Montreal John had no close associates other than James' family; he wanted to share in James' acquired family responsibilities as if they were his own. One is left thinking of John not only as a loner but also a lonely man.

Similarly, it is Andrew's will that gives us an insight into his personal life and character. The document is all the more revealing because it is a holograph, composed not by a notary but by the testator. In 1803, when he was nearly fifty years old, Andrew married a young woman named Ann Wood of Cornwall, Upper Canada. Robert Hamilton, husband of Catherine Askin, wrote to his father-in-law a year later that "[James McGill's] brother Andrew has lately taken to himself a Young Wife, and seems of course perfectly happy,"[16] the usual remark of the casual observer of a May-December marriage. But there are signs in the documents that the union was from the outset not a romantic one. The marriage articles ensuring that the marriage conformed to English and not French law, and therefore declaring the parties to be separate as to property, seem to be unnecessarily insistent that neither the wife nor her family shall have claim upon the estate of the husband if he should predecease her, beyond the £150 per annum promised by the marriage settlement – and even there, the capital is to return upon her death to the Andrew McGill estate. The will itself offers further evidence that the course of the marriage did not run smoothly:

In the Name of God Amen ... And first, to the Supreme Being I most devoutly recommend my Soul, that it may dwell with the Blessed in Peace ...

To the Person who I espoused at Cornwall & my present wife Ann Wood, I have made provision for in the Articles of Marriage of One hundred & fifty pounds Currency per year which is secured to her, to be received after my decease in the 3 per Cent Consols & under the direction of John Brickwood Junr Esqr by a purchase of Stock to amount of Five thousand pounds sterling [sterling crossed out; "stock" written in] – the Interest of which will overpay the Sum that I have agreed for her to receive – And in this my will for reasons best known to myself, I leave to her Three thousand pounds more – not the Capital, but the Interest of it at five per cent after my decease, reserving to myself the power of alteration. In consideration of the distressed state of the [Wood] Family by their being deprived of the Head & Father, I leave to the Mother Mrs Mary Wood Fifty pounds per year, [then follow several small legacies to other members of the Wood family] ...

To my Uncle Ninian McGill of Glasgow if he should survive me Twenty five pounds per year sterling & to my Sister Margaret McGill –

the Interest of One thousand pounds sterling per year & on her decease, to return to the general mass of my Estate – Finally the remainder, whatever it may be, to my Brother James McGill, with all the farms, orchards, Houses, Cattle & Carriages in this Country, whether at Cornwall, Pointe Claire, St Lawrence Suburb & in Town that to me now belongs – signed at my own dwelling House in Notre Dame Street 9th October 1804, Andrew McGill.[17]

So Andrew is more generous than the marriage articles required and obviously has an affection for his wife's family, impoverished by the death of Ann's father, a physician in Cornwall. Ann (who was perhaps about twenty years of age) appeared no doubt to be fortunate in securing this marriage with an affluent Montreal merchant, even if the arrangement sounded somewhat unromantic. But then something went very wrong, and on 22 April 1805 Andrew added a codicil to his will: "In consideration of the very indifferent Behaviour in the conduct of my wife towards me, I have thought it proper to alter the sum of one thousand pounds bequested to her by me in my will to one shilling – the sum by the marriage articles cannot be alterd – Andrew McGill."

However, this fierce addendum (which incidentally has got the amount in question wrong) is now heavily scored out. It was evidently presumed at the time of his death that the scoring out had been done by Andrew, though he did not annotate the codicil to authenticate the deletion; the lawyer who received the will for probate noted the crossing out and accepted the correction as Andrew's – which was very fortunate for Ann Wood, for it meant that her annuity was doubled. A final paragraph appoints James McGill, Isaac Todd, and James Dunlop to be the executors. So Ann Wood's affairs were by the terms of the will in the hands of James, and he seems to have had a personal liking for her. He was, for example, very careful to protect her interests. When he found that the five thousand pounds Ann had in the hands of John Brickwood in England had been consolidated with funds of his own, which were also in Brickwood's care, he wrote at once to say that they must be separated out to ensure that in all eventualities Ann would continue to be paid.

Up to this point, life seems not to have treated Ann Wood very well – her father dying and leaving the family impoverished, her marriage proving unhappy, her husband dying only two years

Bwnside Hall. 1859

When in 1829 McGill's summer estate passed to McGill College; his house became the principal's residence. In 1859 the Montreal High School drawing master made this sketch of boys playing cricket in front of the old farmhouse, which stood on McGill College Avenue, a little above the present de Maisonneuve Boulevard. It was later rented out, then sold to other owners who pulled it down. Artist James Duncan.

after the wedding – but things were going to change for her. Still a young woman and now possessing a yearly income of three hundred pounds, she had become a modest heiress and a desirable prospect. Moreover, she was under the kindly care of her influential brother-in-law James, and, as we shall hear, her life was going to take a very promising turn.

The testimony of the wills, then, is that in family relationships, as in other areas, James was looked upon as the stalwart brother, the one on whom all could depend. The other two brothers readily recognized him as the head of the family and he treated his family responsibilities as seriously, and as generously, as he treated his business and public obligations. But there was no great warmth of affection between the brothers.

Given the paucity of James McGill personal papers, the researcher turns eagerly to the three diaries,[18] more accurately termed calendars, dated for the years 1801, 1802, and 1812. The calendar entries are difficult to read. There is only room for very brief remarks and most are notes on the weather, or the state of the produce at McGill's farm and summer residence, Burnside. He bought this property in lots, as opportunity offered, beginning around 1790. In the end he owned forty-six and a half acres stretching from the lower slopes of the mountain, between what later became University Street and the McTavish estate boundary (which ran fifty yards east of the present McTavish Street), right the way down to the Lachine road (which later became Dorchester Boulevard and is now named for René Lévesque). So it was a typical Quebec-style long narrow holding. But the original farmhouse, which he renamed Burnside Place because a brook ran part way through his land and the name recalled some Glasgow memories, he worked at over the years to make into a very comfortable and pleasant summer retreat. The same Robert Hamilton who remarked on Andrew McGill's marriage visited Montreal in 1804 and wrote back to his father-in-law: "Mr McGill we found in perfect health. To me he appeared as Young as he was Twenty Years ago. In a very comodious country house, about a mile from Town, he seems to possess and enjoy as much Comfort, as generally falls to the Lot of humanity."[19] It is a glimpse of the private James McGill relaxing in the quiet and the beauty of his country home.

But the calendar entries eight years later reveal a different situation. The year began on a note of anxiety: "Jany 1. N.E. wind with sleet and snow. Miss Porteous daily falling off, but free from pain. God help this amiable young Person, her Situation distresses me greatly."[20] Charlotte Porteous, the adopted daughter of the McGills, though she never took their name, was now thirty years of age and revealing ominous signs of consumptive disease. The following month McGill was writing to Askin saying that he fears her illness "will rid [deprive] us of the greatest consolation that either Mrs McGill or I possess." He had already unburdened himself of his fears in a previous letter written three months earlier, so Askin would understand and be able to interpret his terse language:

Miss Porteous, my amiable Miss Porteous, l'*Enfant Chèri* of poor Madelaine, is threatened with decline, and her Situation wrings my heart with woe. Thus must something happen to detach us from the world; all my blood Relations are gone and I fear and dread that this remaining Comfort will also depart. What tie then has this world on me – you will think me melancholy from this Strain, it is not the Case, but I feel poignantly and as I have not Todd nigh me, it is a relief to unbosom oneself to an old Friend, who if he has been less fortunate in life, possesses a Heart of Sympathy and Tenderness not exceeded by any of us.[21]

Here the laconic Scot reveals briefly his deepest emotions. John and Andrew had by now both died, and also, in far off Glasgow, his sister Margaret and his uncle Ninian. He alone was left of all his family. He found after all that deep in his heart something of "auld Scotland" remained. Charlotte Porteous, if not his kin, was of his kith – Scots like himself, as his adopted Canadien family could never be; should she die, he would feel as if his one last link with this life had been severed. The axe he dreaded fell. In his calendar for July he wrote: "1st to 4 weather suny. blowing from w. to n. and east. This morning at 2 o'clock I had the distressing misfortune to lose Miss Porteous by decay."[22]

But the year was 1812, and despite his sorrows, McGill had one more major duty to fulfill before he could lay his burdens down and leave this world for another.

10 In Defence of His City, 1787–1813

For the Canadians of the early nineteenth century, and particularly for James McGill and the merchants of Montreal, the War of 1812 was as unwelcome as it was unnecessary. The immediate causes were straightforward and can be quickly recalled. Great Britain was striving to administer the *coup de grâce* in its long-standing war with France and had instituted a continental blockade of Europe. This created yet another burden for the fur trade, but one that had to be endured stoically. The resulting interference with ocean commerce, however, profoundly annoyed the Americans because it hampered their growing international carrier trade.[1] In enforcing the blockade the Royal Navy assumed the right to stop and search neutral ships for contraband, and infuriated American captains by also claiming that some of their seamen were British subjects (as indeed they often were) and therefore liable to "impressment," that is, forcible enrolment in the British navy. From the American point of view this was nothing other than sheer piracy that had to be resisted at all costs. A belligerent party formed in the Congress, and after much talk the United States finally declared war on Great Britain and its dependencies. But as the Americans were not strong enough to challenge the Royal Navy at sea, the only place where they could attack British possessions was on land, that is, along their own northern frontier. Consequently the Canadians suffered this War of 1812, even though it was not of their doing or of their choosing.

The longer-term implications of the war were more disturbing. Many Americans were by no means unhappy with the turn of events. They had not forgotten that northern frontier line proposed in the 1783 negotiations and still hankered for at least the southern peninsula of Upper Canada to become part of the Union. The area had been settled largely by former Americans, not only zealous United Empire Loyalists but many others who had come north simply in search of free land and lower taxes. Many politicians in the United States persuaded themselves that these Upper Canadians would welcome a liberating army of their former neighbours and fellow citizens. G.F. Stanley has drawn together some of their more disturbing utterances. President Thomas Jefferson himself had remarked that apart from the citadel of Quebec the capture of Canada was "a mere matter of marching." Others were more imperially motivated. Richard Johnson from Kentucky, for example, declared that "the waters of the St Lawrence and the Mississippi interlock in a number of places, and the Great Disposer of Human Events intended these two rivers should belong to the same people," and John Harper of New Hampshire also anticipated the Manifest Destiny doctrine when he said, "To me, sir, it appears that the Author of Nature has marked our limits in the south by the Gulf of Mexico, and on the north by the regions of eternal frost." Even Henry Clay, Speaker of the House of Representatives, wrote in 1813: "It has ever been my opinion that if Canada is conquered it ought never to be surrendered if it can possibly be retained."[2] There can be little doubt that if Canada had succumbed to the American attack, the provinces would have been forcibly and permanently incorporated into the Union. If Canada was fighting reluctantly, she was nevertheless fighting for her life.

Because Upper Canada was the primary target, it was probable that most of the action in this war would take place in the Great Lakes basin and the Niagara Peninsula. Equally probable was that an attack on the St Lawrence valley, if and when it came, would be made as before on the pivotal point of the line – the city of Montreal. So believed James McGill, and mentally and physically he was by no means unprepared for such an assault.

By the year 1811 McGill had, in fact, attained a position of considerable responsibility in Montreal. He was now the senior member of the Executive Council resident in the city; hence in the absence of the governor general and for lack of an elected mayor he was *de facto* the head of civil authority. But he was also colonel and commanding officer of the First Battalion of the Montreal militia. With the outbreak of war he was given two more militia companies and made commanding officer of the garrison of Montreal. Consequently, in this time of crisis, he was the head of both civil and military government in the city.

Potentially the Americans vastly outnumbered the Canadians, and Sir George Prevost, the new governor general and commander in chief of British forces in North America, watching a frontier that stretched from Halifax to the Great Lakes, would have to husband his resources. The Maritime provinces would not be in any immediate danger because of the protection of the Royal Navy and the great difficulties in the way of land access, but the Americans were counting on Britain being so preoccupied with the struggle against Napoleon that she would not have regular army units to spare for the Canadas. In fact, in 1812 Prevost had ten thousand regulars under his command, but of these approximately five thousand were in Nova Scotia, four thousand in Lower Canada, and in the most threatened area, Upper Canada, not more than twelve hundred. These last were under the command of Major General Isaac Brock, who was also the acting administrator of the upper province.

But from his trading contacts, McGill was also aware that there were allies eager to support the British effort. The Indians on the American western frontiers had been given the "treaty" of Greenville in 1795, which had drawn lines between American and Indian territories south of Lake Erie. They were told that all lands south and east of the line were to be open to American settlement, but all those to the north and west were to belong to the Indians.[3] But inevitably the pressure of continued white settlement quickly overflowed these boundaries and Indians led by the Shawnee brothers, Tecumseh and Lolawauchika, were anxious for war to break out between the Americans and Great Britain so that they could have British support in their attacks upon the hated American settlements. The Americans, of course, believed that these Indian attacks were not caused by their own relentless encroachment westward, but were the result of deliberate British encouragement. Where did the Indians obtain their muskets, their powder and shot, other than from British traders out of Montreal? "Who does not know," asked Governor Harrison of the Indiana Territories, "that the tomahawk and the scalping knife of the savages are always employed as the instruments of

British vengeance? At this moment ... their agents are organizing a combination amongst the Indians within our limits for the purpose of assassination and murder."[4]

There was considerable justice as well as rhetoric in these charges. Because the Nor'westers were no more pleased with American settlement in the fur-bearing countries than were the Indians, they readily sympathized with the natives and vigorously continued the Indian trade on which their fur supplies and the native way of life mutually depended. That commerce had always included weapons and ammunition and continued to do so. But at the outbreak of war the partners in the North West Company went further; they not only offered Prevost the services of their ships and men on the St Lawrence and the Great Lakes but also urged him to employ Indians against the American invaders. In addition, they offered to provide stores at what they termed "moderate prices" to the British Indian department.[5] Their offers were gladly accepted. Since the incumbency of Governor General James Craig the administration had been quietly following a dual policy, one public and the other private. "The salient features of both policies were to win the allegiance of the tribes by impressing upon them the wisdom of preserving a friendship with the British in the face of American westward expansion."[6] The secret aspect of the policy had been a generous flow of gifts and strong assurances of military support if war was declared. The British were not seeking a conflict but were determined to make full use of Indian allies if Canada were attacked, and the assistance of the fur traders was essential for the implementation of this policy.

The Nor'westers were, of course, James McGill's former associates and continuing friends. Although by 1810 he had himself retired from fur trading and more recently from general trade, McGill continued to make good use of the merchants' information network. He was greatly alarmed by the increasing American talk of war. His sympathies were naturally with the fur traders and the Upper Canadians, but his immediate concern was with the forces of law and security in his own city, Montreal. He had vivid memories of the American occupation of the city in 1775 and he did not wish that experience to be repeated. His contribution to the defence of his country in 1812 was to be in the preservation of civil peace and good order in the city and in the organization and training of its garrison, the local militia.

These militia units were the third and largest part of the forces under Prevost's command, and if some were ill equipped and poorly trained, there were others that were in a reasonable state of preparedness. In particular Prevost had good reason to be grateful to the local leaders in Montreal. To fill the gap left by the extinction of the feudal obligation laid upon *rentiers* to render military service at the call of their seigneurs, the governor's council had introduced in 1777 the first Canada Militia Act. By this ordinance, all males between the ages of sixteen and sixty were liable for service in the militia of their parish. Failure to enrol invoked fines and the withdrawal of privileges to keep firearms. Captains in each parish had to submit lists of militiamen and to "draw out" their companies on the last two Sundays of June and the first two in July "in order to inspect arms, fire at marks, and instruct them in their duties."[7] James McGill and other prominent merchants had given leadership in this matter for many years. In 1787 that old gossip Alexander Henry, who had been away from Montreal for some time, wrote to a friend: "At my return here I found all our friends Militia Mad, James McGill is a Major and Isaac Todd a Captain and so is old Dobie."[8] Because of his mercantile sources of information, McGill was more aware than most of what was afoot in the United States: he knew they had good reason to be serious about the militia. As early as 1790, a call was issued by the governor general for all officers of the militia to consider urgently "the proper means for putting the Militia under their Command in the most respectable Condition, that they may be able to defend themselves and the Province against all desultory or piratical attacks."[9] In 1794 McGill addressed the grand jury empanelled at the Court of Quarter Sessions in Montreal and took the opportunity to dispel rumours that the militia would be sent abroad to fight wars in distant countries; but, he argued, to go to the assistance of their friends in Upper Canada, if they were attacked, would be only wise and prudent:

The militia ... law was passed for the defence and protection of this province, and not for the defence or protection of distant parts of the Empire; our sister colony of Upper Canada may require our aid, if attacked; we also may require her assistance, under similar circumstances; and is there among us any men, so weak and inconsiderate as to say, we can defend our country when an enemy shall have entered it and no sooner? Shall

GENERAL ORDERS for the
MILITIA of the Province of QUEBEC:
Head Quarters, *Quebec*, 22d. *July*, 1790.

 S the general Protection of His Majefty's Dominions in *America*, in Cafe of a War with *Spain*, may require the Regular Forces in this Province to be withdrawn, and *Canada*, for a Time, be left to her own Defence, common Prudence demands, that all neceffary Meafures be taken to meet that Event.

THE Strength and Exertions of the Inhabitants are the Natural Protection of every Country, and when properly arranged as Militia cannot fail to become its chief and moft permanent Support.

HIS EXCELLENCY THE GOVERNOR therefore recommends to the different Commandants and Officers of the Militia to take all fuitable Opportunities of impreffing the Minds of the People with the Neceffity of Self Defence, as an indifpenfible Duty, intimately connected with the prefervation of their Lives and Property.

THEY will alfo confider of the proper Means for putting the Militia under their Command in the moft refpectable Condition, that they may not only be able to defend themfelves and the Province againft all defultory or piratical Attacks, in the Abfence of the Regular Troops, but alfo, fhould the Safety of the Country render it neceffary, that Competent Detachments from their Numbers may be prepared to join, and act with, the Regular Forces. For this Purpofe it may be advifeable to collect for a limited Time from every Company a proportion of the young Men, that they may be the more eafily trained up and exercifed in the Ufe of Arms, and be more ready to protect their Fellow Citizens from Infult and Interruption in their peaceful Occupations. The Colonels and Field Officers of the feveral Diftricts or Divifions of the Militia are therefore requefted to confult together, as far as Convenience may permit, and digeft the proper Arrangements for carrying this Meafure into Execution, whenever it fhall be found expedient, tranfmitting the Refult of their Deliberations feveraly from each Diftrict to the Adjutant General for His Excellency's Information.

THESE Detachments, when collected and embodied to ferve for a limited Time not exceeding Two Years, will for their greater Eafe and Encouragement receive Pay, Provifions, Arms, and Quarters, in the fame Manner as His Majefty's marching Regiments in this Province, with Cloathing of equal Value, or a Compenfation in lieu thereof.

THE Commandants of the feveral Battalions of Militia weft of *Point au Baudet*, are to tranfmit the Reports for their refpective Diftricts to Sir JOHN JOHNSON Baronet, who will forward the fame to Head Quarters.

By His EXCELLENCY's Command,

FRA. LE MAISTRE,
F. BABY, } A. G.

A call to put the militia in "the most respectable Condition."

we of the town say that when the enemy is at the gates of Montreal it will then be time enough to resort to arms? Or will the inhabitants of a neighbouring parish refuse to assist those, who from local situation may be exposed to inroads from an enemy, until they themselves are attacked in their houses? Surely such language would be equally repugnant to com-

ORDRE du QUARTIER GENERAL de QUEBEC:

Pour la Milice de la Province,

22 Juillet, 1790.

COMME la Protection que Sa Majesté doit en Général à toutes ses Possessions de *l'Amerique*, peut éxiger le départ des Troupes réglées de la Province, et que par là le *Canada* peut être laissé pour un tems à sa propre Défense, il est de la prudence de pourvoir à cet Inconvénient.

C'est la force, ce sont les Efforts des Habitans qui font la Défense naturelle de tout païs; son Soutien principal, et le plus durable est une Milice bien formée.

En conséquence Son Excellence le Gouverneur recommande aux differens Commandans et Officiers de Milice de saisir toutes les Occasions convenables pour imprimer dans l'esprit du Peuple, la nécessité de se défendre soi-même, lui inculquant que c'est là un Devoir indispensable pour la Conservation de sa Vie est de ses Proprietés.

Ils aviteront aussi entre eux des Moyens les plus propres pour mettre la Milice qu'ils commandent dans l'état le plus respectable, afin que dans l'Absence des Troupes cette Milice soit non seulement capable de se défendre elle-même et de se porter promptement dans les endroits où des Attaques passagères et inopinées meneceroient la Province, mais encore pour qu'on puisse aisément en tirer des Détachemens nécessaires qui agiffent de concert avec les Troupes reglées, dans le cas où le Bien du Païs le rendroit nécessaire.

Pour cet Effet il sera peut être à propos d'assembler pour un tems limité un certain Nombre de jeunes Gens à proportion de chaque Compagnie, afin de les discipliner plus facilement et de les exercer au Meniement des Armes, pour qu'ils soient toujours prêts à se porter au besoin et à protéger leurs concitoyens dans leurs paisibles occupations.

Les Colonels et Officiers de l'Etat Major des différents Districts ou Divisions de la Milice sont donc requis de se consulter les uns les autres autant quils le pourront convenablement, pour rédiger les mesures qu'ils auront prises relativement au Projet ci-dessus lorsqu'il sera trouvé expedient d'en venir à l'exécution, pour ce ils transmettront le Résultat de leurs Délibérations à l'Adjutant Général pour que celui-ci en informe son Excellence.

Au reste on promet à ces Détachemens, qui seront levés et incorporés pour servir, une espace de Tems, que ce tems n'excédera pas deux Années, quils recevront pour leur soulagement et encouragement la paie, les Provisions, les Armes et les Quartiers de logement de la même Maniere que les recirvens les Regimens de sa Majesté dans cette Province, deplus un Equipément de Valeur égale; on au lieu d'icelui une juste Compensation.

Les Commandans des différents Bataillons de Milice à l'Ouest de la Pointe au Baudet transmettront les Rapports de leurs Districts à Sir John Johnson Baronet, qui les acheminera au Quartier Général.

Par Ordre de son Excellence,

FRA. LEMAISTRE,   } A. G.
F: BABY.

Appel pour mettre la milice "dans l'état le plus respectable."

mon-sense as to sound policy. Let us then, Gentlemen, by all means in our power, demonstrate to our fellow-subjects a grateful return [i.e., recompense] to the Parent State ... on which it is our happiness to depend, and to whom, when our aid is called for, we owe from interest, from gratitude and from duty, the support of our lives and fortunes.[10]

A bilingual manual was prepared entitled *Rules and Regulations for the formation, exercise and movements of the Militia of Lower Canada*,[11] and while this compendium of military training was not published until May 1812, it shows the seriousness and thoroughness that had characterized militia training in the recent past. James McGill and his fellow officers, because of their personal interest and participation in the militia, proved an important part of Canada's resources when the war finally erupted.

McGill had shown his strong support for the imperial government in other and more direct ways. France declared war on Britain in 1793 and a year later, the same year that he addressed the Grand Jury, James was chairman of the Montreal Association – it was founded in imitation of a similar body in Quebec City and seems to have had no other name – the purpose of which was to support British rule in Canada. The heated revolutionary winds from across the Atlantic were combining with the hot airs from the south to cause considerable apprehension in Lower Canada. In 1799 McGill joined his fellow merchant John Richardson, the fur trader Simon McTavish, and the lawyer Edward Gray in a committee to receive and remit voluntary subscriptions to aid Britain in the prosecution of the war in Europe,[12] and he and his friends waited eagerly for news of the struggle to make its slow journey across the ocean and up the inland waterways. The peace of 1801-03 brought some temporary respite, but with renewal of the conflict the news of Nelson's great victory at Tralgar in 1805 was good news indeed. For the Canadas Britain's command of the oceans was essential. The relieved and grateful merchants of Montreal raised in 1809 a monument to the fallen hero at the top of Jacques Cartier Square, a few yards from McGill's home, and he was a generous contributor.[13]

But if Britain ruled the seas, the land war was by no means won, and the irritation to the Americans was if anything increased. It was ironic that President Madison should sign in Philadelphia the declaration of war against Great Britain on 18 June 1812 when Lord Castlereagh, the new British foreign secretary, had announced only two days earlier in London that the offending naval "stop and search" Orders in Council were to be revoked. But the two men, thousands of miles apart, were ignorant of each other's actions; it would be weeks and months before the news of either decision reached the ships on the high seas and the more distant

Règles et Articles

POUR LE MEILLEUR

GOUVERNEMENT

DE LA MILICE

de la Province du

BAS-CANADA,

lorsqu'elle sera incorporée pour le Service...

Faits et publiés en vertu et sous l'autorité de l'Acte de la 34e. de SA MAJESTÉ.

QUEBEC:

Imprimé par P. E. DESBARATS, Imprimeur des Loix de la Très Excellente Majesté du Roi,

1812.

Rules and Articles

FOR THE BETTER

GOVERNMENT

OF THE MILITIA

of the Province of

LOWER-CANADA,

when embodied for Service.

Made and published under the authority of the Act of the 34th of HIS MAJESTY.

QUEBEC:

Printed by P. E. DESBARATS, Law Printer to the King's Most Excellent Majesty.

1812.

frontiers.[14] In Canada, James McGill, alerted by his private sources, was the first to receive and send to the governor general reliable information that the Provinces were at war. His letter, dated 24 June, 8 A.M., was brief:

May it please your Excellency

I have just been informed by Mr Richardson that he has learnt by an Express from Albany that war has been declared against Great Britain by the American States, and as an Express is going from this [city] to Quebec I hold it to be my duty to give you this Information.

I shall immediately call a meeting of the Executive Councillors [here in Montreal] to consult whether any step should be taken by us in consequence of your Excellencys Instructions, and if any measures should be adopted of an active nature, advice of the same shall be transmitted to you.[15]

McGill signed himself "Chairman of a Committee of the Executive Council," and it is clear that he was acting in accordance with earlier planning. The immediate tasks were to mobilize the militia, decide what to do about United States citizens who were currently present in Montreal and whether immediately to impose martial law, and, finally, what to do about trading relations with the enemy. McGill's correspondence over the next few days and weeks shows that he and his colleagues were grappling with the practicalities of the situation. His fellow councillors in these anxious days, James Monk and Judge P.L. Panet, were old collaborators in public affairs and it is obvious that there was unanimity among them; Panet, although a Canadien, was well known as a strong supporter of the Crown. The order for mobilization of the "embodied" militia was straightway promulgated in the city and dispatched to the captains of militia in the surrounding parishes. Proclamations were also posted that all American citizens must depart the city within a week on pain of arrest. It was decided that for the present it was not necessary to proclaim martial law. When, a few weeks later, it was decided that this step had become prudent, the committee nevertheless recommended that the civil courts should continue until further notice to deal with cases of a purely civil nature.

The question of trade was a more difficult matter. An embargo was placed on the export of articles likely to be of use to the enemy forces, such as arms, ammunition, horse harnesses, blankets, woollens, and scalping knives, and a customs checkpoint was established at the half-way house on the road between La Prairie and St John's on the Richelieu River to enforce these regulations. But merchant that he was, McGill saw no reason for Americans who wanted to continue honest commerce with Canada to be prevented from doing so, especially those bringing in food supplies or valuable export commodities such as lumber or potash. Trade of this kind was to be regulated by the granting of licences, but allowed to continue. Also the petitions of those Americans who asked to be permitted to continue their residence in Montreal were to be scrutinized leniently: "in all doubtful cases," McGill reported to Prevost, "we are inclined to Indulgence rather than Rigour, being of opinion that such are the Intentions of the Governor in Chief." They were further encouraged in this practice, McGill remarks, because, if newspaper reports were to be believed, the United States authorities were behaving with reciprocal "indulgence."[16]

The fact was that enthusiasm for this war was not widespread among the general American population, especially in those States that normally traded freely with the Canadas. Many Vermont and New York farmers saw lucrative opportunities in the need of the British forces to be supplied with grain and cattle. Shortly after war was declared, a clerk in the army commissariat was assigned to oversee the busy trade in beef from Vermont; at Ogdensburg, New York, a constant flow of supplies, mostly cattle and sheep, moved across the St Lawrence to Fort Wellington. When the American commander stationed at Ogdensburg raided Gananoque across the river and provoked a retaliatory raid by "Red George" Macdonell and the Glengarry Light Infantry, compelling the American forces to retreat to Sackets Harbour, the citizens of Ogdensburg petitioned that their troops should not return. Military activities were obviously not good for business.[17] But once war had been declared, raids, skirmishes, even set battles could take place; men could be killed, homes could be and were burned, farms destroyed, women and children massacred.

So war was war; one of McGill's less-difficult decisions concerned the trader named Robert Dickson, who has been described as "the most influential trader in 1812 amongst the western Indians of the upper Mississippi."[18] In the past, McGill had been one of his chief suppliers and indeed had had difficulty in collecting payments. Dickson had been busy on his own initiative distributing presents among the Indians in the name of their Great Father, the king of England, in order to consolidate their allegiance, and then naturally he put in a claim to the army paymaster for reimbursement. This was clearly a military matter and was referred to Major General de Rottenburg, who in mid-July had been assigned overall command of the Montreal district. But Dickson's activities had been, at least ostensibly, in accord with the fur trade's normal patterns and Rottenburg had been instructed to consult with McGill on all commercial matters: to disavow Dickson would be to interfere with the fur trade. So the general called a confidential board to consider whether the trader should be reimbursed and, further, whether he should be encouraged to continue his activities. Present were de Rottenburg himself, Sir John Johnson, the commissioner for Indian Affairs, Isaac Winslow Clarke, deputy commissary general, and, for the fur trade, James McGill, John Richardson, and William McGillivray.

McGill and the other fur traders were hardly unbiased judges in this matter. McGill had already written to Prevost the previous month urging the full use of the traders' services: "The nations of Indians near the Mississippi have hitherto had little or no connection with Government except through British traders who have individually contributed very materially to preserve alive their attachment to Great Britain … [The Indians] are the only Allies who can aught avail in the defence of the Canadas. They have the same interest as us, and alike are objects of American subjugation, if not of extermination."[19] It is not surprising, then, that the committee decided that Dickson's services were of "enormous value" and that he should be both reimbursed and strongly encouraged in his activities. He was recommended for appointment as a government agent with power to employ five officers and fifteen interpreters. These recommendations were approved in Quebec City and implemented. The British and Canadian authorities were more than ready to accept assistance from Indian allies. To do so would further inflame American sentiments and might endanger friendly relationships with American suppliers, but that was a risk that could not be avoided.

McGill's greatest concern continued to be the preparation of the Montreal militia. MacSporran has transcribed his military correspondence for the years 1812-13, and while, as one would expect, most of it is very dull and deals with routine matters such as recommendations for the appointment of officers and their promotions, the letters show that he worked continuously to keep his forces officered, disciplined, and equipped. Shortly before the declaration of war, de Rottenburg, at that time also acting administrator of Lower Canada, ordered the militia officers of the province to consider the best means of mobilizing the "sedentary" contingents. In Montreal, McGill was chairman of the officers' conference and responsible for drafting its report. On 14 June he presented a scheme for dividing the men on the sedentary parish rolls into four groups by age: sixteen to eighteen, eighteen to thirty, thirty to forty, forty to sixty. For the present, drill for six hours weekly should at once be arranged for the second and third groups and the men readied to march at short notice; these would be the "embodied" militia. The other two groups could remain in reserve and form the "sedentary" militia. Arms should be stored in each parish, possibly in the presbyteries – a central, recognized location that did not profane the sanctuaries themselves. These proposals were accepted in Quebec City and put into practice.

A letter addressed to the adjutant general, Lieutenant Colonel de Monviel, provides a good example of McGill's forward planning. It is dated 9 July 1812.

Sir: By the return of the first Battalion of Montreal Militia under date of 5th Instant, you will have seen that the total of Rank and File present is 938 & 27 in Service. Of this Number 236 are returned as Americans Born [and therefore of doubtful allegiance], which would reduce the total number to 729, but as amongst these Americans there are many who from length of Residence & other causes consider themselves & are considered as British Subjects, it may be fairly supposed that, the Men who from age or other disability may not be fit persons to perform Military Duty, will be more than made up for by Americans born, I would therefore take the Battalion as 750 Rank & File. Of those I have allowed the officers commanding the Artillery, the Grenadier & Light Infantry Companies to enroll 100 men for each, and these Companies have volunteered for daily exercise. They have had Three Hundred Stand of Arms. There remains then 450 privates for the eight Battalion Companies, which when equalized will make 56 men per Company. And as they are equally desirous of being trained to the use of Arms with the three Select Companies, I wish to know His Excellency's pleasure, whether he would not allow me to make a Requisition of Arms for the eight Battalion Companies and calling out the whole for training for a Reasonable Time daily, that in the event of Detachments being ordered to march, there may be drawn as nearly as possible a proportion from each Company.[20]

McGill foresaw that the better trained specialized units might be called away to meet the enemy far from Montreal and he wanted to make sure that his city defence force would not be unduly weakened. It is part of the leader's role to look ahead and prepare for possible contingencies.

But it is also his role to take swift and firm decisions when crises arise. As soon as the American declaration of war became known, McGill sought to assemble the embodied militia. This force was to consist of unmarried men, aged eighteen to twenty-five, who were to be enrolled for ninety days, or in the event of armed invasion for one year. The Legislative Assembly of Lower Canada had enacted these terms in February 1812, so McGill had full authority for his call to arms. In a report to the governor general dated 1 July, he wrote that mobilization went smoothly enough, except for resistance "by a great number of the Inhabitants of this Island from the West End of the Parish of LaChine up to the End [of the Island]." Fifty-nine men were called from the area, of whom only twenty-eight responded by crossing over to La Prairie where the troops were being assembled, and of these, four later changed their minds and returned home. The report continued:

With a view of enforcing the Law upon the Deserters and those who never joined, Major LeProhon went on monday into that part of the Division of which he is Major, and accompanied by one or Two Captains of Militia and about Thirty Men, he attempted to carry the Law into Execution and actually apprehended three Men, two of whom are in prison, but the third was rescued by above Two hundred men and many of whom [were] in Arms. Not contented with this insult offered to His Majesty's Government, the Mob threatened that if the two Men who had been sent prisoners to Town were not given up by 12 o'clock today they would come and take them out by force, and further threatened that they would go to LaPrairie and bring away their men who were [already there].

McGill added that the revolt had spread to "St Genevieve behind Pointe Claire," where five hundred men had assembled and expressed the same sentiments: "One of the unlawful assembly declared that they [were] determined upon and prepared for Civil War."

In consequence of this Information and Your Excellency's Instructions of 1st Feby. last The Committee of The Executive Council have considered it to be their duty to adopt a decided line of Conduct, in the hope of putting a Stop to this Spirit of disobedience and outrage. They have come to the resolution of dispatching two confidential Characters to go amongst those mad people to endeavour to bring them to a sense of their duty, by delivering up the Militia Man that was rescued and further to insist that four of the most forward, and who appear to be Ring Leaders in this Revolt, do deliver themselves up to Justice, failing of which to forewarn them of the Consequences and that an armed Force will be sent to seize them.[21]

This force was alerted for despatch the next morning and was to consist of one hundred regulars, two hundred militia, and a detachment of artillery with two field guns. Clearly, McGill was taking no chances. Late in the afternoon, a message from the mutineers said they did not believe the militia law had been passed by the Legislative Assembly, and that they wanted to send a deputation of eight "to confer with those persons who represent the Government," but McGill and his colleagues remained firm and insisted that only the surrender of the culprits would suffice. Otherwise the prepared force would march. Late that evening, a separate troop reinforcement reached Lachine, "which it was expected might deter the mad People from further proceedings," but they refused to disperse "and faced upon the Kings troops"; the soldiers then fired, and the crowd broke and ran, but one person was killed, and three or four wounded. Hearing this, the Committee ordered the larger body to march as planned at daybreak. Consequently, under the command of Captain John Richardson "about 350 men marched this morning before 7 o'clock consisting of English and Canadians nearly equal in number."

The report of this incident is signed by James McGill, James Monk and P.L. Panet, but MacSporran notes that the document is in McGill's handwriting. His language is noteworthy: those who oppose the constituted authorities are "mad people" animated by a "Spirit of disobedience and outrage." McGill learns "with astonishment" that they confronted the King's troops. In response he was not prepared to be lenient or to appear indecisive. This was a war situation, and an enemy attack was imminent. However, he was able to finish his report on a more positive note: "In communicating this unpleasant occurrence, we have much satisfaction in being able to assure your Excellency that the Militia went off [this morning] with great cheerfulness, and that from every Report we obtain there is Reason to believe that, except in the Parishes of Pointe Claire, Ste Genevieve, and Ste Anne, the greatest zeal prevails, and we are of opinion that the prompt measures which have been accepted, will put a stop to further disturbances."[22]

James McGill seems to have gauged the situation rightly,[23] for Alexander Henry wrote to John Askin from Montreal in early October in a most cheerful vein:

We are all soldiers here – I expect preferment [before] the Battle, being the oldest captain in the British Militia. The americans on the opposite side of the river are continually attacking our Boats going up to Kingston, I think it is their intention (if they can) to stop the communication, which they will find a difficult matter to perform. We have near ten thousand men in arms here and can with ease raise twenty thousand more, in ten days in case they come over our lines – but we do not intend attacking them on their side – I hope the Cold weather will disperse them for the Winter, and before the Spring they may have a change in their Government, which will produce a peace … [24]

Henry also mentions that Isaac Todd was in the city and intending to stay the winter, so there was no atmosphere of panic: "We are hourly expecting Genr. Dearboon [sic] with about Ten thousand of his troops to attack us, but we are not afeared of them, as our Canadians are in high Spirits."

One reason for the general mood of optimism at the time Henry was writing was a very unusual event that had recently taken place in the city. Following General Brock's highly successful assault on Detroit, the American general William Hull and his army had been ceremonially received as prisoners of war. This victory greatly boosted Canadian morale, and the carefully staged pageantry in Montreal worked wonders for the local population. The *Montreal Herald* (for the city had three newspapers now)[25] gave a lively and detailed description of the captured general and his troops' reception:

Montreal, September 12th.

... General Hull and suite, accompanied by about twenty-five officers and three hundred and fifty soldiers, left Kingston under an escort of 130 men ... At Lachine Captains Richardson and Ogilvie, with their companies of Montreal militia and a company of the King's [Regiment] commanded by Captain Blackmore, formed the escort till they were met by Colonel Auldjo with the remainder of the flank companies of the militia, upon which Captain Blackmore's Company fell out ... leaving the prisoners to be guarded [as they marched through the illuminated streets] by the Montreal militia alone ... When they arrived at the governor's house [the Château de Ramezay] the general was conducted in and presented to his Excellency, Sir George Prevost. He was received with the greatest politeness and invited to take up his residence there during his stay in Montreal. The officers were quartered in Holmes Hotel and the soldiers were marched to the Quebec Gate Barracks. The general appears to be about sixty years of age and bears his misfortune with a degree of resignation that but few men in similar circumstances are fitted with.[26]

James McGill, as colonel of the Montreal militia and chairman of the Montreal Committee of the Executive Council, was a member of Sir George's entourage in the Château, and Madame McGill and her household had a splendid view of the exterior ceremonies from the windows of her home just next door. It is significant that General Hull, in his official report, attributed the poor showing of his forces to the fear generated in the citizenry of Detroit and among his troops by the large numbers of Indians attached to the Canadian forces.[27]

This initial success was indeed heartening, but it was only that – an initial success. Everyone in Montreal knew that this was not going to be the end of the war and that probably hard fighting lay ahead. Largely owing to the bravery of Tecumseh and his warriors, the Upper Canadians won another important but costly victory in the battle of Queenston Heights on 13 October 1812. They suffered many casualties and lost their outstanding leader, General Isaac Brock. But the enemy suffered even greater losses and was forced to retreat across the river to their own side of the frontier. So the first attack on Upper Canada failed, but for the next twelve months American attacks and Canadian repulses continued. York (Toronto) was burned, but the invaders were cleared from the Niagara Peninsula; the British lost an important naval engagement in Put-in-Bay on Lake Erie, and the Upper Canadians were defeated in an engagement at Moraviantown on the banks of the Thames River. But the Americans could not capitalize on their successes because their troops wanted to return home in time for the harvest. Altogether, from one summer to the next, 1812–13 was an indecisive year, but from Montreal's point of view, it was an opportunity for de Rottenburg and his regulars, and McGill and his militia, to prepare themselves even more thoroughly for the impending assault upon the city.

It was a matter of considerable satisfaction to McGill at this anxious time that the defenders of the city were truly representative of the whole population, both Canadien and British. There were regiments like the Canadian Fencibles that were mainly English speaking and others like the Voltigeurs that were mostly French, and there were the embodied and sedentary militia units drawn from both communities and officered by Canadien or British citizens without distinction. McGill could echo Henry with fervour: "We are all soldiers here."

The Americans did not begin their approach to the city until the fall of 1813. Their plan was to employ a twofold strategy. General Wade Hampton would follow the Lake Champlain-Richelieu route and attack from the south, and General James Wilkinson would advance down the St Lawrence to attack the city from the west. Fortunately for the Canadians, the two American commanders were mutually jealous, each suspecting that in the event of failure the other would attempt to make him the scapegoat. This circumstance alone was of tremendous value to the Canadians. The two invading forces, their every move reported by Indian scouts, slowly and cautiously manoeuvred into position. Having made his way north following the Richelieu, Hampton crossed into Canada as far as Lacolle but then changed his mind, retreated to Chazy, started out again for Four Corners, and from there proceeded down the Chateauguay River. He finally reached Chateauguay itself to the southwest of the city by 25 October. Wilkinson was even more tardy. His army and its boats had not left Sackets Harbor on Lake Ontario until 13 October, and he was still making his way down the St Lawrence, the northern bank of which remained in Canadian hands.

Montreal readied itself to resist the attack. There would be no bloodless surrender as in 1775. Church bells were rung, and beacons lighted to spread the news of the impending danger; all sedentary militia were to report to their captains, even if only armed with axes and spades. James McGill was raised to the acting rank of brigadier general and given command of all the militia forces of the city, a striking confirmation of the respect he had won from de Rottenburg and Sir George Prevost. To borrow Milton's phrase, he was now in Montreal "our Chief of Men."

When news reached the city that Wilkinson's boats had successfully passed Prescott, Lieutenant Colonel Hercules Scott and the 103d regiment of regulars were sent with Indian support from Caughnawaga (Kahnawake) to strengthen Lieutenant Colonel Louis-Joseph Deschambault and the Beauharnois militia already in position at Coteau du Lac, and regular troops under Major General de Watteville were sent to reinforce Lieutenant Colonel de Salaberry's militia companies encamped at Chateauguay, facing Hampton's invasion. De Salaberry's other forces included two companies of his own Voltigeurs, a light company of the Canadian Fencibles, a company of militia from Boucherville and "a handful of Indians." The speed and efficiency with which the militias moved into their positions were especially commendable. William Dunlop, who served as an assistant surgeon in the 89th Regiment and later became a noted Canadian author, wrote in his *Recollections*: "We came up with several regiments of militia on their line of march. They had all a serviceable, effective appearance – had been pretty well drilled, and their arms, being direct from the Tower [of London], were in perfectly good order."[28] Colonel Duguid, in his *History of the Canadian Grenadier Guards*, made a comparable comment: "The obvious ease with which [militia] companies moved and acted in this campaign calls for explanation. There can be no doubt that this resulted from 15 months of consistent training."[29]

As acting brigadier general in command of Montreal's militia defence forces, McGill was kept closely informed on all these military manoeuvres and was called upon to supply local knowledge of the city and its environs, as well as of the qualities of the various militia units and their leaders. Once de Rottenburg and his staff had formulated their plans, McGill passed many anxious days, keeping his men alert while waiting for news of the enemy's approach. He had the satisfaction of knowing that the morale of the population continued to be very high.

For the men of the Chateauguay and Boucherville militias, their day of testing was to be 26 October 1813. That was when Hampton finally mounted his attack on their positions on the banks of the Chateauguay River. The Canadiens were happy to be commanded by one of their own, Charles-Michel de Salaberry, who made expert use of his familiarity with the terrain. He had chosen and prepared his ground with great care, and his main lines stood firm behind hidden wooden barricades and stoutly repelled the American attack. The skilful deployment of flanking militia, to harass the enemy's advance, their expertise in woods warfare, and de Salaberry's example of personal bravery – he stood exposed on a tree-stump, so that he might be seen by all, encouraging his men – were further major advantages favouring the Canadians. Hampton, mired in the swamp into which he had been decoyed, was unable to maintain his communications. In mud and forest the Americans suffered considerable losses and decided to retreat, first to Four Corners, and then from there to Plattsburg. It has been reliably reported that on the Canadian side only some 350 men were actively engaged in this battle, which stopped the march of Hampton's five thousand regulars, but the forward units were supported in depth by many times their own number, had they been needed. Nevertheless, the victory was truly a Canadien-Canadian achievement rather than a British success. It was warmly celebrated in Montreal and by none more unreservedly than James McGill.

But three weeks later, Wilkinson was still coming down the St Lawrence. To better negotiate the Long Sault Rapids, he crossed to the Canadian bank of the river. He was pursued and attacked by British and Canadian forces at Crysler's Farm near Morrisburg. His rearguard was severely mauled, and his main army had to move hastily down river to Cornwall. Fearing further attacks, the Americans decided to recross the river and regroup on their own side at Fort Covington on the Salmon River. Here they learned of Hampton's withdrawal to Plattsburg, and this was enough to persuade them to abandon any further plans for the attack on Montreal. It was the excellent coordination of efforts in Lower and Upper Canada which had proved effective. As George Stanley commented: "What gave Crysler's Farm the appearance of a decisive battle was Hampton's inability to brush de Salaberry's militia aside at Chateauguay."[30] The grand assault on the central pivot of the long St Lawrence valley had been defeated before it could be mounted.

When the early rumours were confirmed that Hampton was back in Plattsburg and Wilkinson in Fort Covington, Montreal could relax. For this city, the War of 1812 was as good as over. Reverting to his substantive rank, Colonel James McGill received a signal from de Rottenburg to stand his militia down and to send his well-deserving patriots back to their homes. He and his men could look back on a job well done; he himself could rest assured he had discharged in full his responsibility for his city and his country. He gave the order for demobilization on 20 November. Four weeks later he was taken sick and after a short illness passed away on the nineteenth day of December 1813. Like Wolfe and Nelson and Brock, he died in the flush of victory.

For the Advancement of Learning

The Gazette published in Montreal on Tuesday, 21 December 1813 included the following item:

Died: On Sunday last, aged 69 years, after a short illness the Hon JAMES MCGILL, one of the members of his Majesty's Executive Council for this province, and Colonel Commandant of the first Battalion Montreal Militia. This venerable and respectable citizen had long and deservedly filled the most elevated stations in his community, both as a Magistrate and Representative in the Provincial Parliament, for which his long residence, his fortune and his talents eminently qualified him, and in the discharge of which he acquitted himself in a manner highly honourable to himself and useful to his country. His remains were interred this day with military honours, and accompanied to the grave by an immense concourse of citizens of all classes, as their last tribute of merited esteem and sincere regret.

Militiaman Robert Cleghorn was a member of the firing party that discharged a farewell salute over the grave of their colonel, and his diary recorded a laconic comment on the weather: it was a day of "Frost, keen, bitter." It is all the more notable that despite the weather the mourners constituted "an immense concourse." In 1797 McGill had taken the lead in the Protestant community's acquisition of a new cemetery, to which he had transferred the remains of his old friend John Porteous, who had died in 1782. In

1813 McGill was interred in the same plot and a monument was erected bearing this inscription: "To the memory of the Honble James McGill, a native of Glasgow, North Britain, and during several years a representative of the City of Montreal in the Legislative Assembly, and colonel of the 4th [*sic*: read 1st] Battallion of the Montreal Militia, who departed this life on the 19th day of December, 1813, in his 69th [*sic*: read 70th] year. In his loyalty to his sovereign, and in ability, integrity, industry and zeal as a Magistrate, and in other relations of public and private life he was conspicuous. His loss is accordingly sincerely felt and greatly regretted." A side panel referred to John Porteous as also being buried there.[1]

What moved so many to honour his funeral was surely that James McGill was the fur trader like no other. Only John Richardson is comparable for his degree of public spirit and genuine concern for Montreal,[2] but he was of a younger generation and had had James McGill as an example to follow. Moreover, he was less generally popular because he had developed a pro-British, anti-Canadien partisanship, which McGill had steadfastly avoided. But apart from these two, the early fur traders did remarkably little for the city that have given them so much. John McGregor published in 1839 a volume entitled *British America* in which he wrote, referring specifically to Montreal: "Those who made their fortunes in the fur trade have nearly, if not all, passed away from the theatre of action, and their money seems to have vanished with them."[3] It was a phenomenon already observable in McGill's own later years, and one that gave him much food for thought.

He discussed the matter with John Strachan. This young man was the schoolmaster from Scotland whom McGill had outfitted and sent upriver to Kingston in 1799. Strachan moved a few years later to Cornwall, where he met Ann Wood, Andrew McGill's widow. James McGill had by no means forgotten his young sister-in-law and was greatly pleased when in 1807 she was courted and married by the schoolmaster, of whom he had already formed a high opinion. During the next few years on his trips upcountry he several times stayed with the young couple, evidently finding their company congenial. On one such visit, he discussed with Strachan this matter of the disappearance of the early fur traders and their immense fortunes, and in a letter written in 1820, Strachan describes the turn the conversation took: "We had been speaking of several persons who had died in Lower Canada and had left no memorial of themselves to benefit their Country, in which they had realized great fortunes. And particularly I mentioned [the need of] a University as the English had no Seminary where an Academical Education could be obtained. We had repeated conversations upon the subject and he departed determined to do something."[4]

In a letter written four years later to the Society for the Propagation of the Gospel in London, Strachan said that when McGill discussed the disposition of his own fortune, the younger man suggested "the propriety of giving by will some assistance for the future education of youth – it would be doing something to the Glory of God and hand down his name with praise to posterity." Strachan added: "Mr McGill relished the hint so well, that he was continually dwelling upon it." According to Strachan, McGill even thought of establishing a college in his own lifetime, but only upon condition that the schoolmaster (who by this time had received ordination and was also the Anglican rector of Cornwall) should remove to Montreal and be responsible for the management of the institution. But this Strachan was not willing to do, and so McGill returned home to draw up his will, and to make provision for an educational bequest.[5]

James McGill's will is notably devoid of any religious sentiment. He had observed the outward forms of religion, and was friendly disposed to all the churches. He displayed a remarkable tolerance at a time when narrow denominationalism was all too prevalent; but there is no evidence that he was personally religious. Strachan had used the phrase "for the glory of God"; McGill, if he had used any such phrase, would more likely have said "for the well-being of the City of Montreal, I bequeath ..." McGill left two hundred pounds each for the Protestant poor of the city, the Catholic poor, the Grey Nuns, and the Hôtel Dieu. These truly were gifts for the well-being of the Montreal community, and we may fairly conclude that in making the college bequest also, McGill was thinking of contributing to the progress of the whole city rather than any particular group. There were in his day no Protestant institutions to provide for (the Montreal General Hospital first opened its doors in 1819), but he did not forget that he had some debts to honour in his native land; thus he gave two hundred pounds each to two public institutions, the Glasgow

Infirmary and the Glasgow Asylum. For many years he had served as Montreal's commissioner for foundlings and the insane. At a time when society was not yet ready to recognize its responsibility for those who were mentally ill, McGill remembered that there were these unfortunates in society and believed they were deserving of charity. His bequests came from the generosity of his heart; they were not consciously "for the Glory of God" but for the well-being of the community – but it is often true that in attempting the one, we most nearly accomplish the other.

The other phrase Strachan had used, "to hand down his name with praise to posterity," had considerably more propriety. McGill in his later years was very conscious that he was a lonely man. Friends, associates, colleagues – these he had, but no close kin. His brothers had died childless before him, two sisters were married in Scotland but their children were not McGills, and he had long since lost touch with the families. He lived comfortably with Mrs McGill and fulfilled conscientiously all the obligations of his own home, especially as regards his step-children, but François and Guy[6] were Desrivières not McGills. He made a rather pathetic gesture towards James Cartwright, eldest son of Richard Cartwright of Kingston, leaving him considerable parcels of land in Upper Canada on condition that he add the name "McGill" to his own "and shall take and bear the family arms of McGill as I the said James McGill do now bear the same," but James Cartwright seems not to have thought the inducement worth the sacrifice.[7] And yet, to depart this world and leave no mark of one's existence? A small college bearing the name "McGill" would at least give a minor immortality.

He had not needed John Strachan to remind him of the need for educational facilities for the English-speaking population of Montreal. That first petition he signed back in 1774 had specifically emphasized the urgency of the matter, and the same concern had been raised many times among his associates in the intervening years.

A year after Chief Justice Smith presented the ill-fated report of his committee on a system of public education, the merchants of Montreal addressed a petition to Carleton in support of Smith's proposals. They wrote somewhat ingenuously: "although your Petitioners from the Infant State of the Province, and their want of Abilities, see great Difficulties and Embarrassments opposed to the Erection and Accomplishment of an Institution so necessary and useful, yet when they contemplate the Benevolence and Patronage of His Majesty, the Assurance of your Lordship's Auspices, the Generosity of the Nation to which they belong ... they look forward with confidence and a pleasing Hope to the Establishment and Completion of an University." They went on to propose that the students should be instructed "in the Learned Languages and Sciences (excepting Theology) and that it may be established on the most liberal Principles and Terms."[8] This "liberality" was, of course, the very thing to which the Roman Catholic bishop was most opposed. But the merchants had overestimated the generosity of the British Crown, and even Carleton's own liberal sympathies were not going to prevail against the negative vote in the forthcoming Legislative Assembly, which the Canadien majority would certainly provide.

Yet the idea of a university would not die. Isaac Ogden, a member of the Quebec administration and like Smith a former New England Tory, produced in 1790 a draft charter for just such a "liberal College." It was to receive a royal charter, have the power to write its own statutes and appoint its own professors (privileges that McGill College did not receive until 1852), and was specifically forbidden to "exclude any Person of any religious denomination whatsoever from equal Liberty and Advantage of Education."[9] It was indeed a very progressive document, far ahead of its times; but James McGill as an executive councillor was well aware of Smith's report and of Ogden's draft and was undoubtedly influenced by them in the carefully neutral wording of his own bequest twenty years later.

He was not the first to think of making a private endowment in an area where the government was so clearly loathe to take the lead. That honour must go to Simon Sanguinet, lawyer, judge, and *seigneur* of La Salle. Sanguinet dictated his will on 14 March 1790, two days before he died. The clause in question reads: "10. Wills and orders that his seigneury of La Salle, water and flour mill, with his house in the city [of Montreal], St Joseph Street, and the ground depending of it, be and belong by charity to the University, which is to be established in this province for the education of youth, on condition that his [Sanguinet's] family will receive free education therein."[10] Unfortunately, Simon's brother Christophe contested the will vigorously, basing his case on the "debility" of the testator at the time the will was drawn. In 1792 Christophe won his case and entered into possession of the estate, so that the bequest was nullified. But the court proceedings were a *cause célèbre*, so much so that, while the matter was still *sub judice*, 175 signatures, Canadien and British, supported a petition asking that the will be enforced; the benefaction at least gave the idea of a university further wide circulation.

So James McGill had available to him a number of earlier proposals to encourage him in his planning, but he realized that in such a large undertaking, the cooperation and goodwill of government was essential. Yet his Canadien friends had erected formidable barriers to any favourable administrative activity: how best could he surmount these obstacles? The Royal Institution for the Advancement of Learning was a good instrument for establishing and overseeing a university, but how to bring the idea out of the social impasse and make it a reality? That was his problem.

McGill was a merchant, and he knew that a solid amount of money and some tangible real estate could often achieve what lofty ideals can only dream. He would leave his country estate for the site of a college, add a sizeable amount of funds to give muscle to his proposals, and leave it in trust to the Royal Institution. This would galvanize the most lethargic of governments into naming the members of the institution (otherwise the bequest would lapse) and the rest he must leave up to them. But he would build into his bequest a time limitation: if the college was not established within ten years of his death, the estate and the endowment would revert to his residuary legatees. It was a shrewd provision.

So together with his lawyer McGill drew up the significant clauses:

I give and devise all that tract or parcel of land commonly called Burnside, situated near the city of Montreal, containing about forty six acres ... to the Royal Institution for the Advancement of Learning, constituted and established ... by virtue of an Act of the Parliament of the Province of Lower Canada made and passed in the forty sixth year of His Majesty's Reign ... upon condition that the said Royal Institution for the Advancement of Learning do and shall, within the space of ten years, to be accounted from the time of my decease, erect and establish ... upon the said last mentioned tract or parcel of land, an University or College, for the purposes of education and the advancement of learning in this Province.[11]

There is no word about who may enrol, what the language or languages of instruction should be, nothing about the subjects to be taught, no word about religion. All that was for the Royal Institution to determine: James McGill wisely left their hands untied. He followed this bequest with a second, endowing the university or college with the very respectable sum of ten thousand pounds. Land and endowment probably added up to around fifteen thousand pounds, or about one-eighth of McGill's estate. He did not mean to fund a whole university; he was only priming the pump and hoped that the government and possibly other well-intentioned benefactors would be prompted to build upon his foundation. There was one other stipulation: if a university should be erected, one college should bear his name; but if only one college should eventuate, it should be called "McGill College."

So James McGill had set a hare running. Probably he would have been philosophical, in the early years following his death, at the lethargy of the government and the tardiness of his trustees, but grateful to John Strachan for lighting a fire under them by pointing out that the years were passing and that the bequests would lapse in December 1823. Probably also he would have found cause for some dry humour, mixed with not a little admiration, at the tenacity of the Canadiens when they passed the Fabriques Act in 1824 and the Syndics Act in 1829, which successively deprived the Royal Institution of any educational responsibilities other than to administer his own bequests, and secured for themselves what they had always wanted, their Church in control of their schools. F.J. Perrault had won out after all.[12] But he would have been saddened by the ingratitude of François and Guy Desrivières, who fought their benefactor's cherished project through the courts, even to the Privy Council in England.[13] But when they finally lost and the estate and endowment were handed over to the Royal Institution, McGill would have been profoundly irritated by the attempts of the Anglican clergy over the next decade and a half to turn McGill College into an ecclesiastical foundation, a pale imitation of Oxbridge in England rather than a sober, workaday institution like his own University of Glasgow. But he would have been cheered when at last, in mid-century, a group of Montreal merchants and professional men – led by James Ferrier, drygoods retailer, promoter of railways, and a keen militiaman, and Peter McGill (a grand name, but no relation), a founder of the Bank of Montreal and also into railways, Hew Ramsay, bookseller and stationer, and Charles Dewey Day, a lawyer and judge, formerly solicitor general for Lower Canada – all solid, practical men, all public spirited like himself, set vigorously about the task of rescuing the college and breathing new life into their great predecessor's project.

He would have rejoiced greatly at all that followed thereafter. He would have been astonished and delighted by the immense contribution of his men of law to the legal and constitutional development of the province; cheered by the achievements of his medical professors and their transformation of the health of his country; greatly impressed by the buildings and bridges and public works of his engineers – and he would have appreciated the fine scholarship and the scientific expertise to be found at the heart of his enterprise, the Faculty of Arts and Science. In his later years he had been a director of the Quebec Agricultural Society – his college, thanks to another merchant, William Macdonald, acquired a whole faculty of Agriculture. James McGill's Montreal had to be a trading city – and here in his college would emerge a fully fledged faculty of Management.

Would he have minded that his modest college grew sturdily into "The University of McGill College" and then, in a new century, into the world-renowned McGill University, with its hundreds of professors, men and women, and its thousands of students, from all the provinces of Canada and from all the lands and cultures and languages of the world? Would he have been hurt that after a hundred years only his name remained, that his own exertions and successes, his own contributions to his chosen country, should have been so soon and so completely forgotten? That the man he had been, that "Chief of Men," was wholly obscured by the vital and immense institution he had fathered?

We think not. He had hoped young James Cartwright might take his name and "bear the family arms of McGill," and so keep alive some memory of his passage through this world. Instead, he was quietly forgotten; but his family name and his Martlet crest are borne proudly all over the globe by the thousands upon thousands of graduates of his university. It still stands on his beloved Burnside estate at the foot of the mountain he revered in the midst of the city and country he chose as his own, administered, defended, and enriched. We think that he lies in deep content beneath the tomb outside the Arts building, and as he hears the many voices of young students passing by, he smiles in his sleep.

Governors and Administrators of the Province of Quebec, 1760–1815

Government and its bureaucracy played a constant role in James McGill's affairs, and readers may find the following listing helpful in the identification of persons' names in the McGill story.

The governors administered the British government's policy for the Province, but at a distance of three thousand miles from London they necessarily had to make many personal decisions. They were assisted by an appointed Executive Committee. In the absence of a duly commissioned governor general, an administrator of lesser rank would be appointed.

1 1760–74
   General Jeffrey Amherst – Military Governor   1760
   1763 Treaty of Paris ceded New France to Britain.
   General James Murray – Military Governor and
   Administrator   1763
   P. Aemilius Irving – Administrator   1766
   General Guy Carleton – first Lieutenant Governor,
   then Governor General   1766–78
   H.G. Cramahé – Administrator while Carleton was
   in England   1770–74

2 1774–91
   Sir Guy Carleton, Governor General
   (remainder of term)   1774–78

1774 Quebec Act defined Quebec boundaries
generously, reintroduced French law, refused
a legislative assembly.

American War of Independence	1775–83
Americans occupied Montreal; attack on Quebec City defeated.	1775
General Frederick Haldimand, Governor General	1778–84
Treaty of Paris redefined Quebec, favouring the Americans	1783
Henry Hamilton – Lieutenant Governor and Administrator	1784
Henry Hope – Governor and Administrator	1785
Guy Carleton, Lord Dorchester, Governor General	1786–96

3 1791–1815

1791 the Province was divided in two, Lower and Upper Canada, and each was given the right to elect a legislative assssembly. In both Provinces an appointed Legislative Council played the role of an upper chamber, having considerable powers of veto. The governor continued to have the assistance of the smaller Executive Council.

Alured Clark – Administrator while Carleton in England	1791–93
Guy Carleton, Governor General (remainder of term)	1793–96
Maj. Gen. Robert Prescott, Governor General	1796
Sir R.S. Milnes, Administrator	1799
Hon. Thomas Dunn, Administrator	1805
Sir James Craig, Governor General	1807
Hon. Thomas Dunn, Administrator	1811
Sir George Prevost, Governor General	1811–15
War of 1812	1812
American attack on Montreal defeated	1813

James McGill died 19 December 1813.

Notes

1 John Michael McGill (1899–1976) compiled a manuscript McGill family history in the 1950s and sent a copy to Principal F. Cyril James, among whose files in the McGill University Archives it is preserved. The history concentrates on Scottish data and does not concern itself with Canadian matters.

2 James II had seven more children after James III. See the family tree, page 7.

3 John Michael McGill draws attention to an interesting illustration of the power of these incorporated guilds to protect their commercial prerogatives. In 1757 James Watt, engineer and instrument maker, wanted to establish himself in Glasgow. He needed only a small facility but was peremptorily refused permission to set up a workshop in the city by the Guild of Hammermen as not being "free of the craft." The writ of the guild did not, however, extend to the university campus, and there he was given a small room in which he designed and constructed a model of a steam engine, the invention that was to provide the major motivating power of the Industrial Revolution. The university still treasures the model, which it owes to the guild's jealous care of its privileges. Even in this century, the guild still retains much of its prestige; when Prince Philip was made an honorary Freeman of the City of Glasgow in 1955, his citizenship was registered in the Incorporated Guild of Hammermen. See "Family History," 11, McGill University Archives.

4 He may well have been the officer of the guild who sent James Watt his dusty answer in 1757.

5 McGill, "Family History," 25, McGill University Archives.

6 The cession was part of a larger deal arranged by Charles I with France in the treaty of St Germain-en-Laye, 1632.

7 At the time of James McGill's birth Glasgow's population was about 20,000; when he first reached Montreal, it had climbed to 30,000; at the time of his death it exceeded 110,000.

8 The term for Canadiens who had taken to the wilderness life of the forests.

9 See Hamilton, ed., *Papers of Sir William Johnson*, XII, 194–5. In an affidavit sworn before the Court of Common Pleas in 1787, McGill referred to "a residence by intervals in this place from the year 1766 until the year 1775, and a constant residence since the last period, being twenty-one years in all." See National Archives of Canada (NAC) 1787, vol. 2, Investigation of Court of Common Pleas; MacSporran, "James McGill," 111, citing ibid.

10 "Mr McGill is described by his contemporaries as a man of tall and commanding figure … in his youth a very handsome man, but becoming corpulent in old age": Principal Sir William Dawson, citing the reminiscences of a "Mr Henderson of Hemison" whom he knew as an old man in his own early years in Montreal. Dawson, "James McGill," 37–9.

CHAPTER TWO

1 This fact alone meant that the fur trade was bound in due course to decline again. Thomas Wien ("Castor, Peaux et Pelletries," 76, especially Figure 3) has shown that while the total volume of the fur trade doubled in the years 1720–90, the proportion of beaver to other pelts declined from approximately one-half to one-quarter. James McGill was one of the first to recognize and respond to the changing circumstance.

2 Glover, ed., *David Thompson's Narrative*, 112–13, quoted by Innis, *The Fur Trade in Canada*, 4.

3 Quoted in Innis, *The Fur Trade in Canada*, 173, citing NAC, Shelburne Mss, L (1754–66), 137–9.

4 Innis, *The Fur Trade in Canada*, 195.

5 Among the voyageurs the "livres" of the French regime were still much in use. It was equal to about seven-eighths of an English shilling, or twenty-two to twenty-three livres to the pound. Lande

quotes Lees, *Journal*, 6: "The wages of the people in Canada in spring 1768 was as follows. A Steersman or Gouvernail out and home Two Hundred livres ... a man in the middle or Ordinary Rower, One hundred and Twenty livres. In former years the wages used to be much higher." Lande, *The Development of the Voyageurs Contract*, 6. Evidently prices rose again, for G.C. Davidson cites Alexander Mackenzie's *Voyages*, published 1801 as saying that a guide, bowman, or steersman would receive from 800 to 1,000 livres for the return journey, Montreal to Michilimackinac, a "middleman" 250 to 350 livres, plus a shirt, pants, and blanket. Davidson, *The North West Company*, 229–31.

6 They were not the first white men to visit the prairies. "The French in 1756 held a chain of forts from Montreal to the Rockies ... After the British conquest these French posts were abandoned ... Soon only slight traces of the civilisation of the French fur trader and missionary were left in the North West." Davidson, *The North West Company*, 33. The nor'westers had to break ground again and eventually went much further.

7 In 1763 there was a brief, violent interruption of the peace by the Indian uprising known as "Pontiac's War," but it was quelled before the main thrust of British trade from Montreal began. The Montreal traders pushing into the Ohio valley lands in the early 1770s also complained of renewed competition from Franco-Spanish interests expanding up the Mississippi from Louisiana; but this never became a major threat to either the Canadian or American trade.

8 His Beaver Club medal bears the date 1770.

9 John's name appears on a list of those subscribing to a declaration of loyalty to the British Crown in 1775; he first appears in Askin's correspondence in 1778, where the reference suggests Askin has heard of John as fulfilling a commission for James at Sault Ste Marie, but has not met him. See Quaife, ed., *Askin Papers*, 1, 125.

10 Innis, *The Fur Trade in Canada*, 196–7.

11 McGill, "Family History," McGill University Archives.

12 James II suffered a considerable loss but retained the Stockwell Street premises. He died in 1789, and the property reverted to his son James, who again sent Andrew, this time with power of attorney, to settle affairs. James continued to be responsible for the upkeep of his sister Margaret and an Uncle Ninian, named in both John's and Andrew's wills, until their deaths, which preceded that of James.

13 The original and three other members' medals are preserved in the McCord Museum of McGill University.

14 He was admitted to the Beaver Club only as late as 1795.

CHAPTER THREE

1 It was opened in 1734. It was six metres wide and ditched on either side, but maintenance was the responsibility of local landowners with varying results.

2 France had ceded Louisiana to Spain in 1762. Initially, the British had drawn a parallelogram on the map of the lower St Lawrence to indicate the area of their military jurisdiction, but this was not intended to mark formal frontiers. The Quebec Act of 1774 defined the western boundary of the province as running due north from the junction of the Ohio with the Mississippi River, but Carleton's instructions from London pushed the boundary further west to the eastern bank of the Mississippi. See map, page 74.

3 The petition "humbly shews That We have lost the Protection of the English Laws ... and in their Stead the Laws of CANADA are to be introduced to which we are utter Strangers disgraceful to us as Britons and in the Consequences ruinous to our Properties as we thereby lose the invaluable Privilege of TRIAL BY JURIES. That in Matters of a Criminal Nature the HABEAS CORPUS ACT is dissolved and we are subjected to arbitrary Fines and Imprisonment at the Will of the Governor and Council." Shortt and Doughty, *Documents*, vol. 1, 414–15. Although James McGill did not sign, his friends Isaac Todd and John Porteous did, and another of the signatories was his brother Andrew, which gives us a date for Andrew's first appearance in Montreal.

4 Simon McTavish, one of the early fur traders and later a founder of the North West Company, refers warmly in a letter of 1774 to a friend in New York to Carleton's part in the drafting of the Quebec Act: "Their present Governor (the first contriver and promoter of this evil) is universally detested." MacSporran, "James McGill," 94, citing North West Company, Papers, Toronto Reference Library.

5 Letter to Hillsborough, 25 April 1770, quoted in Atherton, *History of Montreal*, vol. 2, 44.

6 Atherton, *History of Montreal*, vol. 2, 36.

7 Campbell's was a truly representative force. It consisted of thirty-four regulars, two hundred militia (eighty British, the rest Canadiens), twenty "officers of the Indian Department," and six Indians. They took thirty-six prisoners, of whom sixteen were Canadien, who said they had been assured that the people of Montreal would welcome them without opposition. Stanley, *Canada Invaded*, 46.

8 *Quebec Gazette*, Thursday, 5 October 1775; Historical Section of General Staff, eds., *History*, vol. 2, 85. The list of names also includes John McGill. Andrew's name is missing, but he may have been in Halifax at this time.

9 As a mark of respect for the gallantry of their resistance the defending forces were accorded "the honours of war" and the British officers were allowed to retain their swords. But the whole garrison was sent off to Connecticut as prisoners of war.

10 Allen was sent first to Halifax and thence to London and was finally exchanged for British prisoners on 6 May 1778. He did not fight again in the War of Independence but sought recognition of Vermont as a state independent of New York. Failing in this, he advocated that Vermont become a province in a larger Canada, but died two years before Vermont elected for Statehood within the Union in 1791.

11 It was located at what was later to become the corner of McGill and Notre Dame streets.

12 Atherton, *History of Montreal*, vol. 2, 76.

13 The other signatories were John Porteous (a particular friend of James McGill), Pierre Panet, John Blake, Pierre Mezière, James Finlay, St George Dupré, Louis Carignan, Richard Huntly, François Malhiot, Edward Gray, and Pierre Guy.

14 Atherton, *History of Montreal*, vol. 2, 81.

15 Sanguinet, "Témoin Oculaire," 97.

16 Stanley gives a detailed description of the retreat, 117–33.

17 Franklin made a revealing comment on the Walkers in his report to Congress: they "took such liberties taunting our conduct in Canada that it almost came to a quarrel. I think they both have an excellent talent at making themselves enemies, and I believe live where they will, they will never be long without them." Franklin, *Works*, vol. 8, 182–3.

18 MacSporran illustrates this trait in his character by quoting a remark by Lieutenant Governor Simcoe of Upper Canada in a letter written in 1796 to the British minister in Washington: "The information you require ... is to be gathered from Carver and Hennepin's *Voyages* or rather from the conversation of such a man as Mr Todd." MacSporran, "James McGill," 23.

19 Askin to Todd, 14 April 1812, in Quaife, ed., *Askin Papers*, vol. 2, 705.

20 *Dictionary of Canadian Biography*, vol. 4, s.v. "Guilimin, Guillaume," 318–19.

21 Lighthall, "'James and Andrew McGill Journal,'" 43–50. The "garden of the Jesuits" was attached to the former Jesuit church where the Protestants first worshipped in Montreal and they used the garden as a promenade and gathering place. When the barracks were built it became a parade ground for the garrison and received the name Champs de Mars officially in 1817. After serving for many years as a carpark, it was returned to its promenade status in 1992.

CHAPTER FOUR

1 See Wien, "Castor, Peaux et Pelletries," 76, especially Figure 2.
2 Quaife, ed., *Askin Papers*, vol. 1, 200–2. He reads "promising Friends"; MacSporran, "James McGill," 46, reads "providing Funds," which is no doubt the correct meaning. Alexander and William MaComb were sons of John Gordon MaComb, who like Askin had emigrated from Ireland and spent some years in Albany before moving to Detroit. The sons were very well known among Detroit merchants and acquired large property holdings. Barthe (*sic*) was Askin's brother-in-law.
3 The accepted date is 1779 but these references in Askin's correspondence point to the earlier year.
4 MacSporran, "James McGill," 55. Just as "the West" was a very mobile concept, so too "the North West" was a fluid term. In the 1770s it included an area south of Lake Superior; by the mid-1780s it still referred to the country north of the lake; a decade later it meant areas beyond the Prairies reaching up into Prince Rupert's Land.
5 MacSporran, "James McGill," 52, note 44, citing Superior Court of Montreal Archives, Beek, 119.
6 See Quaife, ed., *Askin Papers*, vol. 1, 84. To make for easier reading, punctuation has been slightly amended.
7 These quotations are from Quaife, ed., *Askin Papers*, vol. 1, 143–4.
8 Catherine Askin, John's daughter, married Captain Samuel Robertson, who was later drowned; she subsequently married Robert Hamilton; their son George founded the town of Hamilton, Ontario.
9 The letter was written 12 April 1786; see Quaife, ed., *Askin Papers*, vol. 1, 235. It is quoted at greater length in chapter 9; see there note 9.
10 Surveyer, "The Early Years of James McGill," 5; from a careful reading of the original somewhat involved letter, it appears that Haldimand had licensed forty trading canoes to go to Mackinac, but Todd, McGill wanted to send an additional four canoes laden with goods to the value of £1,000 for the private use of officers at the post, and also to

send a "batteau" belonging to a M. Campini; but Haldimand would not agree. To seek additional trading opportunities does not seem to justify, on this occasion at least, the use of the word "rapacity," though no doubt both partners seldom let a good business opportunity go by them.

11 MacSporran, "James McGill," 50, quoting letter of James McGill to John Askin, 20 May 1799.

12 Frost, *McGill University*, vol. 1, Index, "Vallières."

13 Lighthall, "'James and Andrew McGill Journal,'" 43–50.

14 See below, Epilogue, and Frost, *McGill University*, vol. 1, Index, "Strachan."

15 The four slaves cost £33.6.8. apiece. A postscript is added to the Todd, McGill account by Pat Langan, acting secretary to Indian Affairs: "The four slaves charged in the foregoing account were purchased by order of the Superintendent-General and Inspector-General of Indian Affairs, in order to fulfil a promise made by Governor St Clair." Surveyer, "Early Years," 9.

16 Askin, writing in May 1778 to a M. Beausoleil at Grand Portage, adds a last casual sentence: "I shall need two pretty panis girls of from 9 to 16 years of age. Please speak to these gentlemen [of the North West Company] to get them for me." Panis was the general name for Indian slaves. Quaife, ed., *Askin Paper*, vol. 1, 98.

17 In a letter to John Askin, dated 20 January 1793; Quaife, ed., *Askin Papers*, vol. 1, 460. The second part of Paine's book had been published in 1792.

18 See Surveyer, "Early Years," 9. There was a marked increased in the number of slaves in Canada when the loyalists began to arrive after 1783, but they were not economically productive in the Canadian climate and by 1804 there were only 142 registered in the Montreal district. Slavery was formally abolished in all British dominions in 1834.

19 See particularly Shortt, "The Honourable John Richardson," 17–27. McGill shared in efforts to found a bank in 1782, 1807, and 1808, but each time the venture failed because the government refused to issue a charter. The Bank of Montreal was finally founded in 1817, but even then had to operate for four years before it received a charter.

20 The McGill cashbook for 1809–15 is even later and offers more of the same kind of information, but in rather less communicative style; it lists credits on the left-hand page and debits on the right, with entries restricted to name and amount. For example, Francis Desrivières and

Thomas Blackwood, McGill's junior associates, each received fifteen pounds a month, presumably as salary. The book was purchased in 1910 by the McGill University library from the Blackwood family, together with some business letters. The letters are in poor condition and difficult to read; they date from 1802–07 and appear to relate mostly to land dealings in the Eastern Townships, and requests for proper deeds to lands accepted from traders Askin and Dickson in settlement of debts. All these financial and business records deserve further specialist study.

21 Lighthall, "'James and Andrew McGill Journal,'" 44–5. "Little A. Todd" was probably the child of Isaac's nephew Andrew Todd, who died in 1797. The boy presumably had come into his great-uncle's care and therefore, predictably, had also become a responsibility of the kindly James McGill.

22 Rare Book Department, McLennan Library, McGill University, CH168.S150. The letter has been lightly edited with regard to punctuation and length. The little girls and the small boy were probably the children of Todd's longtime "housekeeper" who died aged thirty-one and left the children in his care. Isaac freely acknowledged paternity of at least one of the girls. Again, Todd's responsibilities have become McGill's. The trader Dickson or Dixon was another of Todd, McGill's longtime debtors. See below, chapter 10.

23 *Dictionary of Canadian Biography*, vol. 5, s.v. "McGill, James," 528. The Stanbridge acquisition was from Hugh Findlay, Canada's first postmaster general, who acquired it as a Crown grant for meritorious service.

24 This was a pioneering venture into a trade only beginning to become important. Britain's need of lumber to maintain her maritime supremacy became critical in 1808–09, due to the loss of Scandinavian imports. It was met in 1810 by energetic efforts to increase the transatlantic supply. "In 1800 British imports of wood from the colonies were negligible ... 1803, 10,000 loads, more or less; 1808, 66,000 loads; 1811, 175,000 loads." Lower, *Great Britain's Woodyard*, 59, also 71, Table 2.

25 *Dictionary of Canadian Biography*, vol. 5, s.v. "McGill, James," 529. Thomas Douglas, earl of Selkirk, was the great colonizer and inveterate notetaker.

CHAPTER FIVE

1 See chapter 4, note 4.
2 Morris, *The Making of a Nation*, 33.

3 Creighton, *Dominion of the North*, 166–7.

4 Ibid.

5 Stanley, *The War of 1812*, 30.

6 Ibid.

7 In these memoranda, the merchants proposed various alternatives to the 1783 boundary, but their inability to provide maps leaves their verbal descriptions confused. The statements in the text and the accompanying maps reflect their general opinions, and one of their proposals. The other merchants signing the memoranda were McTavish, Frobisher and Co., and Forsyth, Richardson and Co. See Cruickshank, ed., *The Simcoe Papers*, vol. 1, 93–4, 117, 133–7. See also Allen, *His Majesty's Indian Allies*, 57–86.

8 It was truly a matter of great importance. A committee of merchants in Montreal, of whom McGill was one, reported to the Executive Council in 1787 that their total outlay at that time in the "Indian country" was of the order of £300,000. Davidson, *The North West Company*, 19, note 72.

9 McGill does not mean annually but "in the pipeline," "laid out at any one time."

10 Quoted in full, MacSporran, "James McGill," 131. "Great Carrying Place" or Grand Portage, was at the western extremity of Lake Superior and was the major trading post for the Northwest fur trade. Since it proved to be on the American side of the new frontier, it was abandoned in 1802 and the post transferred to Fort William (now Thunder Bay, Ontario).

11 The official headquarters remained in London, England, until 1970, when they were moved to Winnipeg. The chief officers now operate mainly out of Toronto. *Canadian Encyclopedia*, vol. 2, s.v. "Hudson's Bay Company," 843.

CHAPTER SIX

1 McGill, "Family History," 10; McGill University Archives.

2 One of the four "Founding Fathers" of the McGill Faculty of Medicine, Magistrate Dr William Robertson, did just that; when the military fired on the mob and three rioters were killed, Robertson was much criticized, particularly by Louis Joseph Papineau. Magistrate Robertson thereupon challenged Papineau to a duel, which was refused. This was in 1832, almost twenty years after McGill's death. *Directory of Canadian Biography*, vol. 7, s.v. "Robertson, William," 750–2.

3 Neatby, *Quebec*, 49.
4 The Legislative Council was originally a body of eight persons nominated by the Crown whom the governor must consult when enacting legislation. The quorum of this body was five members and this smaller group was known as the Executive Council. When in 1791 Lower Canada received an elected Legislative Assembly, the Legislative Council, increased to fourteen members, became the new upper house. Its members were appointed by the Crown for life. But the governor found it convenient to continue to act in nonlegislative functions by means of an executive body, and the Crown therefore also named an Executive Council, most of whom, but not all, were also members of the Legislative Council. McGill became an acting member of the Executive Council 1793 and a full member a year later. He was nominated to the Legislative Council in 1813 but died before his appointment received royal confirmation. See Shortt and Doughty, *Document*, vol. 1, 704; also Sulte, Fryer, and David, *History of Quebec*, 277.
5 MacSporran, "James McGill," 109.
6 Surveyer, "Early Years," 8.
7 MacSporran, "James McGill," 80, citing Montreal Superior Court Archives, E.W. Gray, Fisbachs and Union Co. Agreement.
8 In 1830, he cooperated with Francis Desrivières in one of the early attempts to construct the Lachine Canal. Frost, *McGill University*, 1, 67, n3.
9 Sandham, *Montreal and Its Fortifications*, 23.

CHAPTER SEVEN

1 While the official political name for the British colony was "the Province of Quebec," the Canadiens and the fur traders continued to call it Canada and used the same term for the land stretching from the gulf of the St Lawrence to the Great Lakes and limitlessly beyond. This usage prevailed even after 1733, until the 1791 act divided "Quebec" into Lower and Upper Canada, and Quebec as a provincial designation disappeared until revived in 1867. But the term "Canada" was still used with both a political and a wider geographic reference.
2 The Americans cancelled reciprocal trading rights in 1816, in the aftermath of the war of 1812, but by that time McGill had been dead three years.

3 Shortt and Doughty *Documents*, vol. 1, 473–4.

4 See chapter 3, note 4, for Simon McTavish's comment in a private letter in 1774 on Carleton's part in the drafting of the Quebec Act: "Their present Governor (the first contriver and promoter of this evil) is universally detested." That attitude still persisted among many of the merchants twelve years later.

5 *Dictionary of Canadian Biography,* vol. 5, s.v. "Carleton, Guy," 141–55. Cf. Wade, *The French Canadians,* vol. 1, 58–9.

6 Carleton arrived at Quebec in November 1786, but McGill was not there to greet him; he had left for England to look after his business interests there. This was the time of the Todd, McGill Company's financial crisis.

7 Shortt and Doughty, *Documents,* vol. 1, 625: "Report of Montreal Merchants on Commerce and Police." The jail was located on Notre Dame Street, not far from McGill's own house.

8 MacSporran, "James McGill," 110–18. McGill's evidence is given in full, citing NAC, 1787, vol. 2, 15 September, Investigation of the Court of Common Pleas.

9 Ibid.

10 He was the old fur-trading companion who died in 1782; McGill arranged burial at his own expense in a grave in the Protestant cemetery. Presumably the lieutenant colonel in this lawsuit was the same John Campbell who effected the capture of Ethan Allen in 1775.

11 Ibid.

12 Dalton, *The Jesuits' Estates Question,* 19.

13 Ibid., 35.

14 Ibid., 47.

15 The Quebec legislature compounded the rights to the estates by granting $400,000 to the Quebec Catholic Education Committee and $60,000 to the Quebec Protestant Education Committee, and the vexed question was finally laid to rest.

16 Shortt and Doughty, *Documents,* vol. 1, 352.

17 Atherton, *History,* vol. 2, 92.

18 See Lareau, *Histoire du droit canadien,* vol. 2, 174–5. The powers of the new Legislative Assembly were of course not absolute; the governor general in council (i.e., the Legislative Council) retained certain veto powers, and matters relating to the military defence and extraprovincial commerce were reserved to the British government. But within

the Province, the Legislative Assembly could and would perform very effectively.

19 In the matter of the assembly, McGill and his friends had now obtained what they had long wanted. But for others, there were serious losses. Fernand Ouellet points out that the new interprovincial boundary effectively cut French Canada off from further western developments. "En établissant une frontière politique à la limite-ouest du peuplement, l'Acte constitutionnel marquait le triomphe du fait culturel et politique sur le fait économique et géographique." Ouellet, *Histoire économique*, 12. It effectively ended the western dream for Canadiens.

CHAPTER EIGHT

1 Quaife, ed., *Askin Papers*, vol. 1, 459.
2 Atherton, *History of Montreal*, vol. 2, 106.
3 Ibid.
4 After he left the Legislative Assembly he continued actively in the Executive Council. In 1813 he was nominated to a vacancy in the Legislative Council but died before the nomination received royal assent from London.
5 Quaife, ed., *Askin Papers*, vol. 1, 488.
6 Memorandum by Bishop Mountain, NAC, Series Q, vol. 74, 207–13.
7 For details, see Audet, *Le Système Scolaire*, vol. 1, 36–8.
8 *Quebec Almanac* (McGill Diaries), vol. 1801, McGill University Archives.
9 Frost, *Dictionary of Canadian Biography*, vol. 7, s.v. "Skakel, Alexander," 809–10.
10 The amount collected was £400, a considerable sum at that time, and Skakel added another £200 of his own money and so acquired an extremely fine range of "philosophical apparatus," which one day he would leave as a most welcome bequest to the young McGill College.

CHAPTER NINE

1 The Committee of Trade was inaugurated in 1822, became the Board of Trade in 1841 and joined with the Chambre de Commerce de Montréal in 1992.
2 MacSporran, "James McGill," 173–90; Adams, *History*; Campbell, *History*.

3 See the Frobisher Diaries in Rare Book Department, McLennan Library, McGill University. The diaries record little but the lists of Benjamin Frobisher's dinner guests.

4 Quaife, ed., *Askin Papers*, vol. 1, 236–7.

5 Ibid., 14, also 441. She enjoyed a happy and fruitful marriage, bearing eight children of whom one, Major John Richardson, spent many years in the British army and subsequently distinguished himself as one of Canada's earliest authors. He wrote the novel *Wacousta, or the Prophecy,* set in the time of Pontiac's War and published in 1832.

6 See chapter 4 above, notes 21 and 22.

7 McGill writes: "I have indeed [no family] of my own, but three girls, of whom two are marrigeable, whom I have brought up." Quaife, ed., *Askin Papers*, vol. 1, 488.

8 James McGill's will. McGill University Archives.

9 Quaife, ed. *Askin Papers*, vol. 1, 235.

10 Ibid., 402–4.

11 Ibid., 487–88.

12 Ibid., vol. 2, 513–15.

13 Ibid., 516. This must be the trader named Robert Dickson, for whom see chapter 10 and note 18 there. Henry spells capriciously and often exaggerates facts; £40,000 probably means "a lot of money."

14 The costs involved in getting a cargo of goods from England to Grand Portage are discussed by the trader Charles Grant in a letter to Haldimand, 1780, whereby it appears that a £300 cargo cost the merchant £750 by the time it reached its destination, but what markup was then added is not mentioned. Ouellet, *Histoire économique*, 107.

15 John McGill's will (copy), McGill University Archives, Acc. 2107/1.

16 Quaife, ed., *Askin Papers*, vol. 2, 425.

17 Andrew McGill's will (copy), McGill University Archives, Acc. 2107/2.

18 See comments in the preface to this work.

19 Quaife, ed., *Askin Papers*, vol. 2, 425.

20 1 January 1812, McGill University Archives James McGill Diary, *Quebec Almanac.*

21 14 February 1812, McGill University Archives (copy). History of McGill Project Files.

22 1 July 1812, McGill University Archives; James McGill Diary, *Quebec Almanac.*

CHAPTER TEN

1 Because of the blockade, "almost the whole of the carrying trade of Europe passed to American ships." Stanley, *The War of 1812*, 16.

2 Ibid., 31–2.

3 Ibid., 22.

4 Cited in Allen, *His Majesty's Indian Allies*, 110.

5 Stanley, *The War of 1812*, 65.

6 Allen, *His Majesty's Indian Allies*, 112.

7 Duguid, *History*, 7.

8 MacSporran, "James McGill," 209; citing "Letters and Accounts of the North West Company."

9 Lande Collection, *General Orders for the Militia*, 1790 (copy), McLennan Library, McGill University.

10 *Quebec Gazette*, 24 July 1794.

11 Lande Collection, *Rules and Regulations for … the Militia*, 1812 (copy), McLennan Library, McGill University.

12 Myron Momryk, *Dictionary of Canadian Biography*, vol. 5, s.v. "Gray, Edward William," 384.

13 McGill and his fellow merchants had a very personal interest. For example, Isaac Todd wrote to John Askin in March 1798 to report the loss to a French privateer of "the richest of our Furr ships," in which "we," presumably Todd, McGill and Co, had furs worth £12,000, possibly one of their last ventures together. Momryk, DCB, v, 818–22, Isaac Todd; Quaife, ed, *Askin Papers*, vol. 2, 135.

14 News of Madison's declaration of war did not reach the American trading post at Astoria on the Pacific coast until 15 January 1813. Stanley, *The War of 1812*, 162. McGill's own information, it should be noted, took a week to get from Philadelphia to Montreal and a further two days to reach Quebec City.

15 MacSporran, "James McGill," 214.

16 Ibid, 219–20.

17 Stanley, *The War of 1812*, 68, 228–30.

18 Allen, *His Majesty's Indian Allies*, 125. For Dickson's trading relations with McGill see chapter 9, note 13. For his importance in mustering Indian allies for the British cause, see Allen, *His Majesty's Indian Allies*, 125–64.

19 McGill to Prevost, 19 December, 1812. Cited in Allen, *His Majesty's Indian Allies*, 151.

20 MacSporran, "James McGill," 224–5.

21 MacSporran, "James McGill," 240–1.

22 Ibid., 242.

23 This is further confirmed by a letter, dated 4 July 1812, from E.B. Brennan, a secretary at "Government House, Montreal" to the chief justice of Montreal, reporting that the miltia had "returned to a sense of their duty" and had promised full compliance with future orders, adding that the "the Magistrates" had consigned only two of their ringleaders to prison. NAC, RG 4, A1, 121.

24 Quaife, ed., *Askin Papers*, vol. 2, 734.

25 First published less than a year earlier, 19 October 1811, the *Herald* had been preceded not only by *The Gazette* but also by the *Canadian Courant* in 1807.

26 Atherton, *History of Montreal*, vol. 2, 117–18; *Montreal Herald*, 12 September 1812.

27 Stanley, *The War of 1812*, 111.

28 Dunlop, *Recollections*, 13–14.

29 Duguid, *History*, 10.

30 Stanley, *The War of 1812*, 265.

EPILOGUE

1 In 1875, when the Protestant cemetery was being closed, McGill's remains were transferred to the McGill university campus, but Porteous was left undisturbed in what was to become Dufferin Square. The original monument was re-erected on campus, but the panel referring to Porteous was turned to present a blank face. In 1944, the McGill Graduates' Society and the Canadian Grenadier Guards jointly marked the Founder's bicentennial with an additional "filial tribute," which is attached to the monument's north side. In 1971, the original sandstone monument had deteriorated to the point where it had to be replaced; "4th Battallion" was corrected to "1st Batalion" but "69th year" was left undetected. See E.H. Bensley, "Is James McGill Buried under the Ginko Tree?" *McGill News* 38 (Spring 1957): 18–19, 45. Also University Archives Fact Sheet, "James McGill's Tomb." For Robert Cleghorn's diary, see Edgar Andrew Collard, "Blink Bonny Gardens," *The Gazette*, Montreal, 12 July 1958.

2 Amongst much else, he was the father of Canadian banking and the driving force behind the founding of the Montreal General Hospital in 1819. He served as its first president.

3 This reference was kindly supplied by Edgar Andrew Collard in a private note.

4 Letter to Royal Institution for the Advancement of Learning, 31 May 1820; Secretary's Letterbook, McGill University Archives.

5 Society for the Propagation of the Gospel, Archives, letter of, 17 April 1824. Strachan went on to become the first Bishop of Toronto and a prime mover in the founding of King's College, which later became the University of Toronto. He continued his interest in McGill College and played a very helpful role in its early critical years.

6 Mrs McGill's grandson was baptized James McGill Guy Desrivières, but he grew up by choice a Canadien and never used his first two names.

7 The titles to these lands appear to have been (like so many others at this time) more than a little dubious.

8 The petition, given in full in Macsporran, "James McGill," 196–9, was dated 31 December 1790; the Assembly was not constituted until fifteen months later, but well in time to ensure that the petition would not be successful. Friends and associates of McGill were among the signatories – for example, John Richardson, Isaac Ogden, P.L. Panet – but whether McGill signed cannot be established for several signatures are now illegible.

9 "Mr. Ogden's Draft for a Charter for a University, 1790," McGill University Archives, 1766 20/1.

10 This Sanguinet was the fervent royalist who had the honour of being arrested in 1776 by General Wooster during the American occupation of Montreal, and who wrote "Le témoin oculaire de la guerre des Bostonnois en Canada dans les années 1775 et 1776." *Dictionary of Canadian Biography*, vol. 4, s.v. "Sanguinet, Simon," 697–8.

11 Will and Testament of James McGill, McGill University Archives.

12 See Frost, *McGill University*, vol. 1, 21–45. Church control was at first exercised at the parish level and extended to administrative levels with the establishment of the Catholic and Protestant Education Committees in 1869. The state resumed full control by means of the Education Act of 1964. See Magnuson, *A Brief History*, particularly "The Triumph of Clericalism, 1867–1900," 39–67.

13 John Strachan wrote to the Trustees: "I should hope that Mr [Francis] Desrivières will have a greater respect for the memory of his greatest benefactor than to contest a Legacy which goes to establish an institution which he had so much at heart." Frost, *McGill University*, vol. 1, 50. Burnside was not conveyed to the Royal Institution until 1829 and the endowment not until 1835.

Bibliography

JAMES McGILL, CONTEMPORARY PAPERS
AND PUBLICATIONS

McGILL UNIVERSITY ARCHIVES
Guide to Archival Resources at McGill University. Vol. 1. University Records.
  1985, Vol. 2. Private Papers, Part 1. 1985. Vol. 3, Private Papers, Part 2.
  1985. Mr Ogden's Draft for a Charter for a University, 1790 (copy).
Quebec Almanac for years 1801, 1802, 1812, containing terse handwritten
  notes by McGill.
Two letters, McGill to John Askin and to Isaac Todd, 1812. Photocopies.
Will and Testament of Andrew McGill (copy, 1804).
Will and Testament of James McGill 1811 (copy, 1813).
Will and Testament of John McGill (copy, n.d.)
The Daybook of the James and Andrew McGill Company 1797–1814.
Four documents concerning Burnside and its boundaries, 1798 and 1803.
Quebec Gazette, 27.07.1794; Address to Montreal Grand Jury, 8 July 1794,
  by James McGill (photocopy).
Secretary's Letterbook (1820), Royal Institution for the Advancement of
  Learning. 39 pages.
Surveyer, E. Fabre, "James McGill, 1744–1813," *La Presse*, Montreal,
  August 1927. Typescript. 17 pages.
"McGill Family History," John Michael McGill. Unpublished ms. N.d.
History of McGill Project Files, B 2.0 through B 12.5.

RARE BOOK DEPARTMENT, McLENNAN LIBRARY,
McGILL UNIVERSITY LIBRARIES

James McGill's Cashbook, 1809–15.

Deed of conveyance of land, formerly city fortifications, 1805 (copy).

James McGill's executors' cashbook, 1813–25.

Frobisher, Joseph. Diaries, 1806–10.

Frobisher, Joseph. Papers concerning the McGill estate, 1810–34.

General Order for the Militia, 22 July 1790 (Lande Collection).

Letter, James McGill to Isaac Todd, 17 October 1805.

MacSporran, Maysie Steele. "James McGill: A Critical Biography," 324
  pages. MA thesis. McGill University, 1930.

NATIONAL ARCHIVES OF CANADA

Memorial upon the Indian Trade to his Excellency Guy Carleton, Esq., 20
  September 1766.

Letter, Guy Carleton to Colonial Secretary Lord Hillsborough, 28 March
  1770.

Letter, James McGill to Lieutenant Governor Henry Hamilton, 1 August
  1785.

Investigation of the Court of Common Pleas, September 1787.

Petition of Citizens to Governor General Lord Dorchester, 31 December
  1790.

Memorandum of Bishop Jacob Mountain to Administrator Sir Robert
  Milnes, 1799.

Letter, James McGill to Governor General Sir George Prevost, 24 June
  1812.

Letter, James McGill to Governor General Sir George Prevost, 1 July 1812.

Letter, James McGill to Governor General Sir George Prevost, 2 July 1812.

Letter, E.B. Brennan, secretary at Government House, Montreal, to the
  Chief Justice of Montreal, 4 July 1812.

Letter, James McGill to Lieutenant Colonel de Monviel, Adjutant General,
  9 July 1812.

Letter, James McGill to Governor General Sir George Prevost, 19
  December 1812.

METROPOLITAN TORONTO REFERENCE LIBRARY

North West Company. Papers, 1763–1803.

SOCIETY FOR THE PROPAGATION OF THE GOSPEL ARCHIVES, LONDON

Letter from John Strachan to the Society, 17 April 1824.

REFERENCE BOOKS

Canadian Encyclopedia. 3 vols. Edmonton: Hurtig, 1985.
Dictionary of Canadian Biography. Edited by George Brown and Francess Halpenny. Toronto: University of Toronto Press, 1966–
Historical Atlas of Canada. Vol. 1, to 1800. Edited by R. Cole Harris. Vol. 2, 1800–91. Edited by R. Louis Gentilcore. Toronto: University of Toronto Press, 1987, 1993.
Historical Atlas of Canada, 3d ed. Edited by D.G.G. Kerr. Don Mills: Nelson, 1975.

SECONDARY SOURCES

Adams, F.D.A. *History of Christ Church Cathedral Montreal.* Montreal: Burton's, 1941.
Allen, R.S. *His Majesty's Indian Allies, 1774–1815.* Toronto: Dundurn Press, 1992.
Atherton, W.H. *History of Montreal.* 2 vols. Montreal: Clarke, 1914.
Audet, L.-P. *Le Système Scolaire de la Province de Québec.* 4 vols. Québec: Éditions de l'Érable, 1950–1952.
Bensley, E.H. "Is James McGill Buried under the Ginko Tree?" *McGill News* 38 (Spring 1957): 18–19, 45.
Bishop, Morris. *White Men Came to the St Lawrence.* Montreal: McGill University Press, 1961.
Campbell, R. *History of the St Gabriel Street Church.* Montreal: Drysdale, 1887.
Collard, E.A. "Blink Bonny Gardens." *The Gazette,* Montreal, 12 July 1958.
Craig, Gerald. *Upper Canada, 1784–1841.* Toronto: McClelland & Stewart, 1963.
Creighton, Donald. *Dominion of the North.* Rev. ed., Toronto: Macmillan, 1957.
Cruickshank, E.A. *Simcoe Papers.* 4 vols. Toronto: Ontario Historical Society, 1923.
Dalton, R.C. *The Jesuit Estates Question, 1760–1888.* Toronto: University of Toronto Press, 1968.
Davidson, G.C. *The North West Company.* Berkeley, CA: University of California Press, 1918.
Dawson, William. "James McGill and His University." *The New Dominion Monthly* (March 1870): 37–9.
Duguid, A. Fortescue. *History of the Canadian Grenadier Guards, 1760–1964.* Montreal: Gazette Printing Company, 1965.

Dunlop, W. "Recollections of the War of 1812–14." *Literary Garland,* new series, vol. 5, Montreal, 1847. Edited by A.H.U. Colquhoun. Toronto: Historical Publishing Co., 1905.

Franklin, Benjamin. *Works,* 10 vols. Edited by Jared Sparks. Boston, 1844.

Frost, S.B. *McGill University, For the Advancement of Learning.* Vol. 1, 1801–93. Montreal: McGill-Queen's University Press, 1980.

Glover, R., ed. *David Thompson's Narrative of Travels in Western North America, 1784–1812.* Toronto: Champlain Society, 1962.

Hamilton, M.W., ed. *Papers of Sir William Johnson,* 14 vols. Albany, NY: University of the State of New York, 1957.

Henry, Alexander. *Travels and Adventures in Canada and the Indian Territories, 1760–76.* [New York, 1809.] Edited by M.M. Quaife. Chicago: Donelly and Sons, 1921.

Historical Section of General Staff, eds. *History of the Organisation, Development and Services of the Military and Naval Forces of Canada.* Vol. 1. The Local Forces of New France, the Militia of the Province of Quebec, 1763–1775; Vol. 2, The War of the American Revolution, the Province of Quebec under the Administration of Governor Sir Guy Carleton, 1775–1778; no publisher, no date.

Innis, H. *The Fur Trade in Canada.* Rev. ed. Toronto: University of Toronto Press, 1956.

Lande, L.M. *The Development of the Voyageurs' Contract.* Privately published. Montreal, 1989.

Lareau, E. *Histoire du droit canadien.* 2 vols. Montreal: Librarie Générale de droit et de jurisprudence, 1899.

Lees, John. *Journal.* Edited by C.M. Burton. Detroit: Society of the Colonial Wars of the State of Michigan, 1911.

Lighthall, W.D. "The Newly Discovered 'James and Andrew McGill Journal, 1797.'" *Trans. Royal Society of Canada* 24 (1935): 43–50.

Lower, A.R.M. *Great Britain's Woodyard, British America and the Timber Trade, 1763–1867.* Montreal: McGill-Queen's University Press, 1973.

Macmillan, Cyrus. *McGill and Its Story, 1821–1921.* London: John Lane, 1921.

Magnuson, R. *A Brief History of Quebec Education.* Montreal: Harvest House, 1980.

Macgregor (M'Gregor), John. *British America.* Edinburgh: William Blackwood, 1839.

Mackenzie, Alexander. *Voyages from Montreal ... with a Preliminary Account ... of the Fur Trade.* [London, 1801.] Edited by J.W. Garvon. Toronto: The Radisson Society of Canada, 1927.

Morris, R.B. *The Making of a Nation*. New York: Time Inc., 1963.

Neatby, Hilda. *Quebec, the Revolutionary Age, 1760–1791*. Toronto: McClelland & Stewart, 1966.

Ouellet, Fernand. *Histoire économique et sociale du Québec, 1760–1850*. 2 vols. Montreal: Éditions Fides, 1971.

–*Lower Canada, 1791–1840*. Toronto: McClelland & Stewart, 1980.

Quaife, M.M., ed. *The John Askin Papers*, Vol. 1, 1747–95. Vol. 2, 1796–1820. Detroit: Detroit Public Library Commission, 1928, 1931.

Sandham, A. *Montreal and Its Fortifications*. Privately published. Montreal, 1874.

Sanguinet, Simon. 'Le témoin oculaire de la guerre des Bostonnois en Canada.' In *Invasion du Canada, 1775–76*, edited by H.A.B. Verreau. Montreal: Senécal, 1873.

Shortt, A. "The Honorable John Richardson." *Canadian Bankers' Journal* 29 (1921–22): 17–22.

Shortt, A., and A.G. Doughty, eds. *Documents Relating to the Constitutional History of Canada*. Vol. 1, 1759–91. Vol. 2, 1791–1818, edited by. A.G. Doughty and D.A. McArthur. Ottawa: King's Printer, 1914.

Stanley, G.F.G. *Canada Invaded, 1775–1776*. Toronto: Hakkert, 1973.

–*The War of 1812*. Toronto: Macmillan, 1983.

Sulte, Benjamin, Charles Fryer, and Laurent David. *History of Quebec, Its Resources and People*. Vol. 1, 1534–1867, Vol. 2, Biographies. Montreal: Canada History Company, 1908.

Surveyer, E. Fabre. "The Early Years of James McGill." *McGill News* (September 1929): 1–11.

Wade, Mason. *The French Canadians, 1760–1967*. Toronto: Macmillan, 1968.

Wien, Thomas. "Castor, peaux et pelleteries dans le commerce canadienne des fourrures, 1720–1790." In *Le Castor Fait Tout*, edited by Bruce Trigger, Toby Morantz, and Louise Dechêne. Fifth North American Fur Trade Conference, 1985. Montreal: Lake St Louis Historical Society, 1987.

Index